Porträts von
Selbstporträts u
Othe

project space

10. Juli – 28. August 2007

July 10 – August 28, 2007

 Verlag für moderne Kunst Nürnberg

James Ensor Haus (Detail), Oostende, Belgien 2000

Inhalt | Contents

Vorwort

Nur oberflächliche Menschen urteilen nicht nach dem äußeren Erscheinungsbild. Das Geheimnis der Welt ist das Sichtbare, nicht das Unsichtbare.

Oscar Wilde

Paul Albert Leitner hat zweifellos ein Auge für die Geheimnisse des Sichtbaren. Er stellt es in all seiner kruden Beschaffenheit vor und reist mit dem Betrachter seiner Werke durch die Welt. Der Realismus ist frappant, aber keinesfalls kühl dokumentarisch, vielmehr artifiziell überhöht durch akkurate Inszenierung. So legt sich eine zweite Realität über die offensichtlich sichtbare und offenbart deren anderes Gesicht: ein komisches, grausames, begehrendes oder dekadentes. Die durch Komposition, Fokus und Farbe eingetretenen scheinbaren Verzerrungen des Realen dienen der poetischen Vertiefung und Analyse von Welt.

Für die Ausstellung im project space der Kunsthalle Wien hat Paul Albert Leitner drei Werkkomplexe ausgewählt, die das Porträt thematisieren: *Porträts von Künstlern und anderen Personen* sowie *Selbstporträts und Natur*. Leitner lässt seine Porträtierten posieren, manchmal so, wie sie sich selbst sehen, manchmal nach seinen Anweisungen. Komposition, Licht, Schatten, Gewandung werden abwechselnd zu wichtigen Attributen, die den Porträtierten eine ungeahnte Realität verpassen, jene, die Paul Albert Leitner als die ihre erkennt oder gerne als deren anderes Ich imaginieren möchte. Dann tauchen auch

Porträts mit der eigentümlich trockenen Bezeichnung „Porträts von anderen Personen" auf. Es sind Bekannte, Unbekannte, Personen, die der Künstler auf seinen Reisen oder auch nur in Wien trifft und die er meist in einer aus dem Rahmen fallenden Form fotografisch festhält. Die dritte Gruppe bilden die *Selbstporträts und Natur* – Porträts des Künstlers der letzten 25 Jahre mit Naturausschnitten als Pendants dazu. Jeweils ein Naturbild offenbart uns etwas über den abgebildeten Künstler auf seinen Entdeckungsreisen durch die innere und äußere Welt. Wir erkennen einen Künstler, wie er sich in der Außenwelt inszeniert und einen, wie er sich in der Intimität von Hotelzimmern meist, in einer Form der Selbstbeobachtung, bewegt.

Es sind dies Diaprojektionen, die ein wenig dem Medium nahekommen, das den Künstler magisch anzieht: dem Film, untermalt mit Musik, die ihn und seine Fotografien ein Leben lang begleiten. Das Moment des Verweilens hat die Diaprojektion dem Film voraus und so wird Kontemplation möglich. Daneben zeigt Paul Albert Leitner noch Farbfotografien aus seiner Serie der *Selbstporträts und Natur*.

Paul Albert Leitners ungebrochene Suche nach einem Bild der Gegenwart gerade in entlegeneren Regionen, an der Peripherie, macht ihn zu einem Archäologen einer im Verschwinden begriffenen Welt. Er zeigt uns in schonungsloser Offenheit die brüchige Realität von Städten, die einerseits von der Globalisierung überholt werden und die auf der anderen Seite vor unseren Augen verfallen: Archäologien ehemals blühender Städte, die versinken, und Menschen, die diesem Rhythmus erliegen oder von ihm überrollt werden. Dieser entblößende

Blick erinnert uns oft an den von Leitner so verehrten Boris Michajlov, obwohl jener die Dokumente einer verrückten Welt durch seine Form der Empathie noch grausamer erscheinen lässt.

Paul Albert Leitner hat eine Affinität zu der Welt des Remoten, des erschreckend unwirklich Realen. Das Remote bedeutet auch das Hängen an einem Zustand der angehaltenen Zeit, eines Raumes im Schwebezustand. Der Künstler – selbst ein skurriler Mensch, der aus einer anderen Zeit zu kommen scheint und doch diese aktuelle Jetztzeit in so präziser Weise zu lesen vermag – zwingt den Fluss, zum Stillstand zu kommen und er verweigert jede Form der Frenetik des modernen Lebens und der digitalen Technologien. Ermöglicht wird diese Position durch seine Distanz als ein Beobachter, der außerhalb steht und doch immer wieder wie ein Reporter die Widerstände des Realen zu spüren bekommt – dann, wenn ihn die Polizei oder andere aufhalten, weil er gesehen hat, was er nicht sehen durfte, obwohl ihn an jenem Sujet vielleicht nur ein ganz spezielles unwichtiges Detail interessierte, das von Poesie sprach, nicht von kruder Realität…

Ich möchte Paul Albert Leitner für sein ungebrochenes Engagement in der Ausstellungsvorbereitung danken und ich freue mich, seine Arbeit der letzten drei Jahrzehnte zumindest mit einem Ausschnitt aus seinem umfassenden Archiv würdigen zu können.

Danken möchte ich auch Sabine Folie (Kuratorin), die dieses Projekt zusammen mit dem Künstler und dem Team der Kunsthalle Wien vorangetrieben hat: Martina Piber (Produktion) und Robert Gebauer (Technik) – ein Projekt, das für den Künstler einen weiteren Schritt auf seiner Reise bedeutet, deren Übertitel stets lautet: „Kunst und Leben. Ein Roman".

Gerald Matt
Direktor Kunsthalle Wien

Paul Albert Leitner
Von einem der auszog … den Künstler als jungen Mann zu porträtieren.

Sabine Folie

Der Künstler, der hier beschrieben wird, zieht nicht aus, um „das Gruseln zu lernen". Aber er hat etwas von dem unerschrockenen Blick des Jünglings in Grimms Märchen, dieser Resistenz gegenüber dem Erkennen von potenziellen Gefahren auf seinen Reisen. Die Unerschrockenheit bewirkt paradoxerweise, dass die Gefahren sich zurückziehen und sich enttarnen als Schimären der Einbildungskraft. Alle monströsen Begegnungen, die jeden anderen in die Knie zwingen würden, können dem jungen Mann nichts anhaben, aber es gruselt ihn am Ende vor einem Eimer kalten Wassers mit Fischen darin.

Dem Künstler eignet dieselbe eigentümlich selbstbezügliche Naivität und Unerschrockenheit wie dem Jüngling im Märchen: Alle realen und surrealen Vorkommnisse auf seiner Reise werden hingenommen, beseitigt, akribisch mit der

Kamera festgehalten, vorerst ohne großartige emotionale Beteiligung. Wovor ihm gruselt, was dem lakonischen Chronisten, seinem inneren Kichern, den Schauer über den Rücken jagen könnte, wissen wir nicht. Vermutlich etwas Kleines, Unscheinbares, von dem wir nie erwartet hätten, es könnte Parodisten der großen Gefühle und Poeten der „Realität des niedrigsten Ranges" (Tadeusz Kantor) aus der Bahn werfen. Dennoch: der Künstler und Beobachter der Welt durch das Medium des Porträts seiner selbst hält uns nicht nur auf Distanz, um in seinen absichtsvollen Gebärden bewährte und verkommene Ausdrucksgesten von Jahrhunderten vorzuführen, er lässt uns über das Äußere der *Natur* durchaus in die Gefilde seines Innenlebens vordringen. Dort, in den Pendants zu seiner physischen Erscheinung, führt unser Künstler das Naturbild ein. Es dient in dieser diptychonen Juxtaposition als Ergänzung, als andere Perspektive des ausgestülpten Ich: Es ist Seelenspiegel. Dieses Innere ist schreiend rot, dicht, verworren, die ruhige See, ein abgebrochener Ast, ausgefranste Palmen, Vögel in der Abenddämmerung – die ganze Palette empfindsamer Metaphorik.

Immer *wird dennoch in meinem Blick*
unsichtbar eine Rose des Bedauerns sein,
wie wenn der Schatten eines Vogels
über einen See strich.

Philipp Jaccottet, *Bäume*

Alfred Stieglitz betrachtete seine Wolkenbilder zwischen 1925 und 1931, die *Equivalents,* als Ausdruck seiner emotionalen Befindlichkeit zum Zeitpunkt der Aufnahme. Ihre Darstellung sei geeignet, eine ebensolche Empfindung beim Betrachter auszulösen.

Diese Entwicklung, Natur und Welt generell als ein System von Entsprechungen zu sehen, als sich gegenseitig reflektierende Kräfte und nicht als normative, absolute Gegebenheiten, nimmt schon im 18. Jahrhundert ihren Anfang, als die Kunst und die Geschichte als gewordene sich selbst zu reflektieren begannen, als die Helden des klassischen Zeitalters verschwanden und die Strategie, nicht in verzweifelte Melancholie zu verfallen, die der Einfühlung war. Friedrich Schillers Rezept: „Das Gegentheil der naiven Empfindung ist nehmlich der reflektirende Verstand, und die sentimentalische Stimmung ist das Resultat des Bestrebens, auch unter den Bedingungen der Reflexion die naive Empfindung, dem Inhalt nach, wieder herzustellen. Dieß würde durch das erfüllte Ideal geschehen, in welchem die Kunst der Natur wieder begegnet.“[1]

Wenn wir uns von diesen Augenweiden der Seele wieder zurückbegeben zu den Darstellungen des Künstlers „he, himself", dann sehen wir einen Flaneur zwischen Welten. Wenn er sich aufmacht, ferne Orte zu erkunden, nimmt er seine unabdingbaren Requisiten mit – darunter den Anzug. In Iran, Kuba oder Argentinien ist er kolonialistisch weiß, in Rumänien, Persepolis, Novgorod oder New York darf er grau sein, auch mit Hut – schelmisch kommentiert in *Selbstporträt (romanesk)*, *Dachterrasse des Hotel Palace, Constanta*, 2001. Der Kommentar „romanesk" verweist auf den Charakter der Nachstellung,

---

1 Friedrich Schiller, *Schillers Werke*, Nationalausgabe, Bd. 20: *Philosophische Schriften*, 1. Teil, Weimar 1962, S. 473

Selbstporträt (romanesk),
Dachterrasse des Hotel Palace,
Constanta, 2001

der Travestie, der Authentizität simuliert, so tut als ob: „Ich ist
ein anderer" – romanesk, rumänisch eben. Die Bezeichnung
impliziert schon, dass es sich um eine exotistische Praxis
handelt: eine Praxis der Aneignung und Überzeichnung, der
Typologisierung, ein Charakteristikum des Burlesken: „...der
augenfälligen Charakteristik wegen bevorzugt die Burleske
starre Typen. Der Trunkenbold, der tölpelhafte Bauer, der
ruhmredige Soldat und der Geizige sind gleichartig stets wie-
derkehrende Figuren."[2] Gleichzeitig ist der Begriff romanesk
eine Art Neologismus, weil aus der Fremdsprache übernom-
men (romanesc); eigentlich bedeutet romanesk aber episch,
romanhaft ausladend: das Leben – ein Roman.

Hier nun, in den offensichtlichen Selbstporträts, unter-

---

2 Wilhelm Fraenger, *Formen des Komischen*, Dresden/Basel, 1995, S. 37

scheiden sich die Sichtweisen auf das eigene Selbst: intim oder distanziert. Die intimen, meist im Hotelzimmer, nackt, mit Handtuch, Turban *à la Marat,* oder in der Dusche, kommen dem berühmten Blick in den morgendlichen Spiegel gleich: etwas melancholisch, sezierend, schamhaft, nicht immer in vorteilhafter Perspektive, scheinbar unbeobachtete Blicke auf den Rücken des Protagonisten und dann der beliebte Topos des multiplizierenden Blicks in den Spiegel mit Kamera – das Paradigma des Selbstporträts als Fotograf, ergänzt durch einen noch tieferen Blick in die Seele, seitlich versetzt im Seelenkörper Natur: sattes Fuchsia der Bougainvilleas, die vor Aufruhr und Begehren beben, oder blau-grünliches Pastell als Hintergrund für schwarze Schattenklekse, ein tachistisches Meer der Unbestimmtheit … Ein System der Korrespondenzen und Paraphrasen: Jacob Burckhardt würde von Äquivalenten sprechen, von kompositorischen Prinzipien, die im Bild Akzente, Bedeutung und Ausgleich schaffen: Hier suchen vertikal aufragende, horizontale oder diffuse Linien und Konturen in der *Natur* des Öfteren eine signifikante, formale, metaphorische Entsprechung im *Porträt*.

Der Künstler fotografiert sich also im Spiegel: lakonisch, kokett oder ernst, gar pathetische Gesten imitierend und daher oft karikaturenhaft. Die Spiegelselbstbildnisse der Künstler befragen besonders seit dem 17. Jahrhundert ihren Status als Dokumentaristen des Wirklichen und Illusionisten des Idealen. Ihr Selbstbildnis, oft sogar, wie bei Annibale Carraccis *Selbstporträt auf der Stafflei* (1604), eines, das sie gerade selbst fertiggestellt haben und als solches in das Bild stellen, hat die Funktion der Selbstreflexion. Victor I. Stoichita spricht vom selbstbewussten Bild oder von der auktorialen Einfügung durch den Spiegel: „Damit der Maler sein Werk, das Machen dieses Werks und sich selbst darstellen kann, muss er eine *schize* imaginieren und annehmen: zugleich *im* Tableau und *außerhalb* zu sein, ,er selbst' zu sein und gleichzeitig ,ein anderer'. In den theoretischen Traktaten über die Kunst wird diese *schize* thematisiert. Samuel van Hoogstraeten macht daraus eine Regel, die für jeden ,Historienmaler' gültig sei: er müsse gleichzeitig Akteur in seinem Bild und Zuschauer der Darstellung vor dem Bild sein. Dem [...] Moment des ,Zweifels' (,man kann nicht zugleich *im* Gemälde und *außerhalb* sein, sondern nur entweder da, oder *hier*') entspricht eine Suche nach den Möglichkeiten der Spaltung. Diese Suche manifestiert sich vor allem in der Weise, wie die instabile und fluktuierende Beziehung, die innerhalb des gespaltenen auktorialen Ich zwischen dem ,Ich' und dem ,Anderen' besteht, behandelt wird."[3] Was für die Malerei gilt, gilt dem Prinzip nach ebenso für die fotografischen Selbstbildnisse mit Spiegel, von denen die Kunstgeschichte seit der Erfindung der Fotografie viele kennt. Wenn dieses forschende Ich nun wieder aus der *schize* heraustritt, sehen wir erneut das andere ICH vor uns: den extrovertierten, eingekleideten Künstler. Der Blick der Distanz.

Es gibt eine sture Persistenz, eine unschuldige und gleichzeitig clever-gewitzte Hartnäckigkeit, strenge Rituale zu befolgen, mondän weiße oder graue, etwas altmodische Anzüge anzuziehen und in diesem Aufzug oder auch halb bis kaum bekleidet sich in Pose zu setzen. Der Selbstauslöser determi-

---

3 Victor I. Stoichita, *Das selbstbewusste Bild. Vom Ursprung der Metamalerei*, München 1998 (1993), S. 268

niert das Zeitmoment in diesen gefrorenen Gesten. So sehr der Künstler die Position austüfteln muss, um sich dann schnell in die richtige Position zu bringen, so sehr wirkt die Pose kaum verhohlen von übertriebener Gekünsteltheit. Die Ergebnisse dieser Bemühungen entbehren daher einer nicht ganz unfreiwilligen Komik, da sie oftmals, historische Vorbilder imitierend, karikierend, diese letztlich verfehlen und das Pathos der *Tableaux vivants*, wie sie im 19. Jahrhundert zur Bildung des Geistes nachgestellt wurden, sich in ein manchmal grotesk-dekadentes Zitat eben dieser historischen Vorbilder in Malerei und Skulptur oder des Fotografen selbst verwandeln.

Waren schon *jene Tableaux vivants* im bereits erwähnten Bewusstsein der eigenen Historizität, obwohl Pathos affirmierend, selbstreflexiv inszeniertes Nachdenken, so ist nun *dieses* Zitieren, meist im Modus der Burleske, eine noch weiter gehende Form der Darstellung des Verlusts der großen Form und der großen, bedeutsamen Geste. Die von Aby Warburg in den dreißiger Jahren des letzten Jahrhunderts so emphatisch untersuchten *Pathosformeln* kippen genau in jene Sphäre der Überzeichnung, des „Superlativen", wo der Ausgleich zwischen den Grenzwerten im Augenblick „der höchsten Erregung (pathos) oder tiefster Versenkung (ethos)"[4] misslingt und in die Karikatur abgleitet. Warburg sah die Gefahr bereits in der barocken Kunst gegeben, jener Zeit im 18. Jahrhundert, die Werner Busch so kenntnisreich in *Das sentimentalische Bild. Die Krise*

---

4 Aby Warburg, Festwesen [Mappe mit Notizen zwischen 1903 und 1906], S. 79, zitiert nach Ernst H. Gombrich, Aby Warburg. *Eine intellektuelle Biografie*, Hamburg 2006 (1970), S. 230

der Kunst im 18. Jahrhundert und die Geburt der Moderne als Periode des Umbruchs schildert.

Gilbert & George, obwohl von unserem Künstler verehrt, nur vermeintlich Wesensverwandte, weisen das Moment der Ironie strengstens von sich und halten es eher noch mit dem Ideal der Pathosformel. Aus den *Living Sculptures* als ontologischem Erkenntnisprinzip soll sich das Wesenhafte, die Essenz der wahren Motivationen, der inneren Regungen aus der angehaltenen Bewegung destillieren lassen: „I think that what we have in all the pieces, from the beginning to the end, is this image of people standing still, as still as possible in the world. Frozen. Not too much walking. We want them frozen for ever. In all our images we have that. We have these images of us, people, human beings, who have been frozen. Because only when they are frozen can you look at them. If they start running you cannot look at them. We want to make them more and more still, and more and more you can actually look at them. You can look inside them."[5]

Bloße Ironie wäre allerdings auch für unseren Künstler die falsche Kategorie: Zuviel der Reflexion würde dem manchmal staunenden Don Quichote angesichts der Seltsamkeiten, die ihm allenthalben begegnen, seine Unschuld nehmen.

Die Pedanterie in der Auswahl der Farben, des Sujets, des Ausschnitts, der formalen und kompositorischen Beschaffenheit stellen sich vor jede emotionale Beteiligung. Diese ist, wenn vorhanden, ins Komische verzerrt, mit der ironischen Distanz des Zitierenden, ob es nun Davids *Tod des Marat*

5 Gilbert: „Interview with David Sylvester", in: *The Rudimentary Pictures*, Milton Keynes 1998, o.S.

Jacques Louis David, Tod des
Marat, 1793

Selbstporträt im Spiegel,
Paris 1996

(1793), Tischbeins *Goethe in der römischen Campagna* (1787),
Mantegnas perspektivisch verkürzter *Toter Christus* (1480)
oder ein Dante mit Lorbeerkranz mit elegisch angeschnitte-
nem Profil ist. „Die *Parodie* hält scherzhaft die vornehmen Formen des verspotteten Urbildes bei, doch durchsetzt sie den
adligen Aufwand da und dort durch triviale Einzelheiten",[6]
belehrt uns der Forscher des Komischen, Wilhelm Fraenger.
Die Reminiszenzen an das Vorbild sind mehr oder weniger
evident, aber meist von ihrem erhabenen Sockel gestoßen ins
menschlich Triviale oder ins Elegisch-Nostalgische, wenn wir
die zahlreichen Szenen betrachten, in denen der Protagonist
auf dem Bett hingestreckt todesähnlich liegt.

Es stellt sich kein *punctum* ein – nach Roland Barthes

6 Fraenger, a.a.O., S. 56

Johann Heinrich Wilhelm
Tischbein, Goethe in der
Campagna, 1787

Selbstporträt, Forum
Romanum, Rom 1999

17

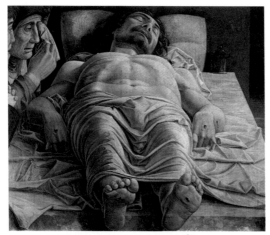

Andrea Mantegna, Toter Christus, 1480

jenes Ergriffensein durch ein Moment des Zufalls –, das den Betrachter trifft, ihn berührt. Der Künstler hat es nicht auf Einfühlung, das Sentimentalische angelegt, obwohl es manchmal durchzuschimmern scheint. Die Lehrjahre des Gefühls enthält uns der Protagonist vor; wir können sie erahnen, da uns die fotografische Anamnese immerhin 25 Jahre zurückführt und den „Künstler als jungen Mann", nicht sehr heldenhaft, mit umgehängter Decke und Sonnenbrille in den Swimmingpool führt. Dort steht er bis zu den Knien im Wasser und könnte wohl kaum zum Objekt der Begierde für David Hockney werden. Jahre später steht derselbe Anti-Held in weißem Anzug auf dem Trampolin am Swimmingpool, das fotografische Pendant zeigt dieselbe Szene – der Held ist verschwunden – mit Hund, der sich auf das Sprungbrett zubewegt. Vom Porträt

„Me, Myself in a Hotel",
Gramercy Park Hotel,
Suite Number 1521, Manhattan,
N.Y.C. 2002

eines Künstlers als junger Mann zum Porträt des Künstlers als Hund – diese Art der Selbstironie liegt dem schalkhaften Künstler. Ganz anders Gilbert & George, die er manchmal in seinen gefrorenen Gesten mehr zu parodieren als zu zitieren scheint: „We are living sculptures. All the good ones for us are living monsters, like Van Gogh. He became a living sculpture. Don't you think even Rembrandt became a living sculpture, or Francis Bacon became a living sculpture?"[7]

Es handelt sich bei unserem Künstler um eine Profanisierung des Heiligen, des Erhabenen oder auch um die Rückholung der großen Geste, die nicht mehr angebracht erscheint, brüchig ist, höchstens als Parodie überlebt. Dieser Raum des Erhabenen ist

---

7 Gilbert & George, in: *The Rudimentary Pictures*, a.a.O.

Selbstporträt mit
Lorbeerkranz, Wien 2000

ausgeforscht und es scheint, als bliebe kein Rest für den Künstler, sich darin würdevoll zu geben, weil die Lächerlichkeit auf der Lauer liegt und jeden Ansatz von Pathos zerstreut.

Der Künstler schreibt also auf seinen *empfindsamen Reisen* ein Reisetagebuch im fotografischen Medium. Er registriert damit die Verwandlungen, die er im Laufe seiner Lebensfahrten erfährt. Ganz in der Tradition der empfindsamen Reise eines Lawrence Sterne und seiner *Sentimental Journey through France and Italy* (1768) und der zahlreichen nachfolgenden Entwicklungsromane durch Reisen begibt sich der Künstler (als junger Mann) auf die Reise in sein Ich. Seine Wahrnehmung verläuft über die autobiografische Form seiner äußeren, physischen Existenz, der *die Natur* im Diptychon als Spiegel der Seele gegenüber tritt. Läuterung sollte die Erfahrung der äußeren Welt bringen, ganz im Sinne von Goethes *Italienischer Reise* (1786) oder Tiecks *Franz Sternbalds Wanderungen* (1798).

Reisen dieser Art gibt es seit dem Beginn ethnographischer Forschung nicht mehr. So räsoniert Claude Levi-Strauss in *Traurige Tropen* (1955): „Nie wieder werden uns die Reisen, Zaubertruhen voll traumhafter Versprechen, ihre Schätze unberührt enthüllen. Eine wuchernde, überreizte Zivilisation stört für immer die Stille der Meere. Eine Gärung von zweifelhaftem Geruch verdirbt die Düfte der Tropen und die Frische der Lebewesen, tötet unsere Wünsche und verurteilt uns dazu, halb verfaulte Erinnerungen zu sammeln."

Diesem Wissen um die Unmöglichkeit der Unschuld und des Nostalgischen steht die Verzerrung im hilflos Lächerlichen gegenüber. Die Karikatur ist das Resultat. Es gibt keinen Platz für Empfindsamkeit: Die Logik des Globalen steht dem brüchigen Selbst schroff gegenüber, als wäre Letzteres ein Relikt aus vergangenen Zeiten – ob es sich aufgeräumt, stramm im Anzug gibt oder weich und verletzlich aufgelöst im halbnackten Zustand.

Vielleicht ist die Musik das einzig wirklich Nostalgische – die Musik vergangener Zeit, die den Künstler und seine Bilder begleiten als Erinnerungsresonanzkörper und Füllung eines theatralischen Raumes, der nahezu filmisch wird. Sie spendet tröstliche Ermattung und dann und wann vielleicht eine kleine Ekstase…

Der Dokumentarist mit dem surrealen Blick.
Paul Albert Leitner im Gespräch mit Gerald Matt

Gerald Matt: Sie sagen immer: „Die beste Geschwindigkeit des Fotografen ist die Schrittgeschwindigkeit." Ist Langsamkeit ein wesentlicher Bestandteil Ihrer künstlerischen Strategie?

Paul Albert Leitner: Ich denke schon! Es ist meine Haltung. So bin ich. Die Altersweisheit signalisierte mir eines Tages, dass Geschwindigkeit eine Schimäre und der sogenannte Turbokapitalismus etwas Lächerliches ist. Sport hat mich vielleicht deshalb nie richtig fasziniert, weil nur der Wettkampf gegen die mechanisch gemessene Zeit zählte. Wie die Marschallin in Hofmannsthals *Rosenkavalier* philosophierte, was der Quantenphysiker Anton Zeilinger sagte oder Albert Einsteins Gedanken, dass der Umstand der Geschwindigkeit von der eigenen

Bewegung oder auch in welchem Gravitationsfeld man sich befände abhänge – über die Zeit und deren Ablauf –, darüber ist an anderer Stelle bereits gesprochen worden![1]

Ich bin immer mehr der Betrachter. Betrachtungen und Beobachtungen erfordern Zeit. Ich stehe am Rande und zweifle. Vor der Masse muss ich mich schützen. Man denkt da immer unweigerlich an Schafherden.

„Nutzt die Zeit; denn die Tage sind böse" (Epheserbrief). – Aber zurück zur Fotografie und zur Langsamkeit der Zeit. Meine Motive – auf dem Lande wie auch in den Städten – müssen erwandert werden. Das ist auch sehr oft mit physischen Schmerzen verbunden. Mit Schmerzen und Geduld. Manchmal mit Glück. Das Glück des Zufalls. An dieser Stelle möchte ich eine Passage aus der Neuen Zürcher Zeitung vom 19. Mai 2007 notieren, exakt zu diesem Thema „Langsamkeit". Dort las ich einen Satz von Benjamin: „Das Labyrinth ist die Heimat des Zögernden." Hartmut Böhme folgerte: „Der Flaneur sucht nicht den schnellsten Weg von hier nach dort, sondern bevorzugt die Odysseen des Zufalls." Wie zutreffend doch für mich und meine Arbeitsweise. Leider fällt mir auch noch ein zu erwähnen, dass es heute zunehmend schwerer wird, durch die Straßen von Städten zu flanieren. Der Grund sind die wildgewordenen Radfahrer auf „Radwegen", für die ganz einfach die Gehwege halbiert wurden.

G.M.: „Mein Ohr steht auf der Straße wie ein Eingang", soll Robert Musil einmal gesagt haben. „Mein Auge steht auf

---

1   Siehe dazu: Interview Gerald Matt mit Paul Albert Leitner im Ausstellungskatalog *Vertigo*, Ursula Blickle Stiftung, Kraichtal. Triton Verlag, Wien 2001

der Straße wie ein Eingang", könnte Paul Albert Leitner sagen. Oder irre ich mich?

P.A.L.: Beide Sätze treffen auf mich zu, aber in anderer Anordnung und meistens erst in Folge einer vorangegangenen Bewegung, nämlich des Durchschreitens der Straße mit dem Auge. Wenn ich einen für mich neuen Ort erkunde, ist mein Auge zuerst ein im Schritttempo sich bewegender „Eingang", der nur dann stehen bleibt, wenn sich ihm eine Situation oder Konstellation zu erkennen gibt, die er in sein Archiv eintreten lassen möchte. Das geschieht dann mittels meiner Kamera. Manchmal ist diese Situation mit Geräuschen verbunden, die zum Bild dazugehören. Ich nehme diese Geräusche dann mit dem Diktaphon zusätzlich auf. Das Reifenquietschen bremsender Linienbusse in New Yorks Madison Avenue klingt wie ein avantgardistisches Musikstück. In einem solchen Moment stehen also mein Auge wie auch mein Ohr auf der Straße „wie ein Eingang". Später mache ich aus diesen kombinierten Aufnahmen Dia-Ton-Collagen.

G.M.: In der Ausstellung im project space sind mehrere Bild- und Sound-Collagen installiert. Was gibt es da zu hören?

P.A.L.: Die Ausstellung besteht aus drei thematisch gruppierten Diaprojektionen mit je 80 Bildern sowie einer Auswahl an Abzügen, die ich an einer Wand installiere. Für diese spezielle Situation ist es mir wichtig, eine Atmosphäre zu schaffen, die sich dem Medium Film annähert. Daher verwende ich diesmal keine O-Ton-Aufnahmen vom Diktaphon, sondern stelle eine eigene Collage aus mehreren Musiktiteln zusammen, Musik, die ich oft und gerne höre. Das wird ein Mix aus Worldmusic, Jazz, Klassik – Maria Callas, meiner Lieblings-Opernsängerin, Ibrahim Ferrer, Frank Sinatra und anderen. Mit dieser Musik wird der Ausstellungsraum akustisch unterlegt, während die insgesamt 240-Dias über die Wände takten. Ich mache ja keine Filme, aber ich liebe den Film und das Kino als atmosphärischen Raum.

G.M.: Außer einer Serie von *Selbstporträts*, die auf vielen Reisen entstanden sind, werden wir auch *Portraits von anderen Personen* zu sehen bekommen. Da sind Persönlichkeiten wie John Gossage, Shirin Neshat oder Katarzyna Figura dabei, aber auch anonyme Figuren. Wie entstehen diese Portraits?

P.A.L.: Der eigentliche „Übertitel" meiner fotokünstlerischen Arbeit lautet seit vielen Jahren: „Kunst und Leben – ein Roman". Ein wichtiger Teil meines Lebens findet auf Reisen statt. Wo ich gerade bin, sehe ich Dinge, passieren Situationen und Momente, die ich fotografiere. So begegne ich auch den Menschen, die ich porträtiere. Das können mir unbekannte Personen auf der Straße oder im Kaffeehaus sein, die ich fotografisch festhalten möchte, aber eben auch international bekannte Künstler oder Musiker zum Beispiel, auch Kuratoren und Museumsleiter. Manche kenne ich schon vorher, hatte mit ihnen zu tun durch meine Ausstellungen, die ja oft auch Gruppenausstellungen sind, andere sind mir nur namentlich bekannt. Niemals „jage" ich irgendwelchen „Stars" nach, um sie in meine Sammlung einzubringen, sondern sie begegnen mir. Meine Porträts sind daher auch keine Schnappschüsse, vielmehr bedarf ein Porträt einer Einwilligung des Porträtierten, bevor die Fotografie entsteht. Wenn Sie gerade die bekannte polnische Schauspielerin Katarzyna Figura nannten: Ich verbrachte die Silvesternacht zum „Jahrtausendwechsel" im Grand Hotel Sopot an der polnischen Ostseeküste. In einem überfüllten Café in Sopot setzte sich ein Paar an meinen Tisch, das waren Katarzyna und ihr Freund Kai. So lernte ich sie kennen. Ein Jahr später begegneten wir uns in Warschau wieder.

G.M.: Ihre Porträts wirken oft wie inszeniert, sei es durch die Haltung der Personen oder durch bestimmte „Requisiten". Wie lässt sich bei einer zufälligen Begegnung während einer Reise so innehalten, dass eine Art „Studioaufnahme" ohne Studio entstehen kann?

P.A.L.: Das „Studio" ist die jeweils vorhandene Umgebung, der ich manchmal auch ein „Requisit" entnehme, ein farbiges Tuch oder eine stachelige Kastanie. Objets trouvés sozusagen. Wie schon gesagt, ist ja die Person damit einverstanden, dass ich sie porträtiere. Dadurch folgt sie meinen Regieanweisungen oder inszeniert sich selbst spontan mit. Meistens gilt – wie bei Helmut Newton – der Grundsatz: don't move! Das betrifft aber nur den Moment der Aufnahme, des Abdrückens. Das „Bild" entsteht schon vorher, in meiner Vorstellung, die sich unter Berücksichtigung der Umgebung verfestigt, bevor mit der Inszenierung begonnen wird. „Umgebung" bedeutet nicht unbedingt den ganz konkreten Ort, an dem ich die Person angetroffen habe, sondern eher das weitere Ambiente dieses Ortes. Manchmal finden sich dort klischeeartige Hintergründe wie eine Terrasse mit Fernblick oder eine Dämmerungsstimmung. Überhaupt ist das Licht sehr wichtig für die Inszenierung, die Atmosphäre und die Bildkomposition, die sich aus Licht und Schatten ergeben kann.

G.M.: Welche Rolle spielt für Sie das *Tableau vivant* in diesem Zusammenhang? Reinszenieren Sie Zitate aus der Kunstgeschichte? Bei Ihrem Selbstporträt im Forum Romanum denken wir ja unwillkürlich an Tischbeins Goethe-Porträt. Oder der Tiroler Sammler Lothar Tirala, der wie eine One-Minute-Sculpture des Bildhauers Erwin Wurm posiert …

P.A.L.: Ja [lacht], das ergibt sich manchmal wie von selbst. Leitner als Goethe in Rom, das war natürlich ganz bewusst als Zitat inszeniert. Das Porträt von Tirala dagegen ist 1997 entstanden, in Instanbul, da wusste ich noch gar nichts von den situativen Inszenierungen Erwin Wurms. Manchmal stellen sich bei mir aber auch spontane Assoziationen ein, ich paraphrasiere dann ein mir im Kopf befindliches Bild. Klemens Ortmeyer habe ich zum Beispiel im Profil abgelichtet,[2] so dass nur ein Auge zu sehen ist wie in dem Fotoporträt, das Irving Penn 1957 von Pablo Picasso gemacht hat. Picassos Auge blickt bei Penn aber den Betrachter an, während Ortmeyer eine Sonnenbrille trägt. Es sind dies also keine eigentlichen *Tableaux vivants*, die

---

2   In diesem Katalog ist ein anderes Motiv abgebildet als das hier beschriebene.

ich da inszeniere, wenn mir ein vorhandenes Bild einfällt, es geschieht dies eher assoziativ.

G.M.: Paul Albert Leitner im Hotel: ein immer wiederkehrendes Sujet. Das Hotelzimmer als „Studio" zwischen New York und Montevideo …

P.A.L.: … oder als spezielle Bühne für meine Selbstporträts auf Reisen. Auf alle meine Reisen nehme ich meinen eierfarbenen „Fotoanzug" mit, und immer gibt es in diesem Anzug ein Selbstporträt im Hotel. Ich halte dadurch einerseits einen momentanen Zustand, eine Befindlichkeit fest und schaffe andererseits ein Dokument meiner Existenz. Indem ich immer im selben Anzug auftrete, zeige ich auch auf, dass es bei meiner Arbeit nicht so sehr um die Orte geht, an denen ich mich befinde, sondern um das Thema „Kunst und Leben": Als Romanfigur tauche ich da und dort auf, und ein Hotelzimmer bedeutet soviel wie einen temporären Aufenthaltsort, ein kurzes Innehalten während der Passage. Ich nenne diese Selbstporträts *Me, Myself in a Hotel*. Dahinter steckt übrigens wieder ein Zitat: ein Bild von Max Beckmann aus dem Jahr 1922 mit dem Titel *Selbst im Hotel*.

G.M.: Wenn wir dasselbe Bild meinen – ich kenne zumindest eine Lithografie gleichen Titels –, dann raucht Beckmann dort eine Zigarre. Bei Ihnen taucht das Motiv des rauchenden Porträtierten auch häufig auf.

P.A.L.: Früher war die Zigarette ja praktisch ein fixes „Attribut" des Künstlers, ein Zeichen für Individualität, Unabhängigkeit, Selbstbewusstsein. Dann haben fast alle geraucht, die Zigarette war nichts Besonderes mehr. Heute aber werden Raucher ausgegrenzt, „Raucher fügen sich und ihrer Umgebung nachhaltige Schäden zu", steht auf jeder Zigarettenschachtel. Die Selbstdeklaration als Raucher auf einem Porträt hat heutzutage also wieder eine besondere Dimension. Daher interessiert mich dieses „Motiv", auch wenn ich persönlich nur ganz selten rauche. Ich „sammle" aber auch andere Motive, wie zum Beispiel Goldzähne im lachenden Mund eines Menschen oder rot gefärbte Lippen – da geht es natürlich auch sehr stark um die Farbe, um Akzente.

G.M.: Ihre Bilder erscheinen mir auch wie eine Sammlung von Gedankensplittern, Kurzreportagen, Fragmenten und Essays aus einer Welt, die wir zu kennen meinen, die wir aber so noch nicht gesehen haben. Empfinden Sie sich als Geschichtenerzähler?

P.A.L.: Die Welt bietet viele faszinierende Geschichten an: verrückte, komische, schaurige, quälende, melancholische. Die fotografischen Motive sind kleine Fenster in die Welt, visuelle Splitter. Mir liegt das Fragmentarische sehr. Fragmente einer fremden Stadt, exotische Pflanzen, die Schönheit einer desolaten Steckdose im Hotelzimmer, das Erbrochene einer fremden Person auf der Straße, eine frisch überfahrene Taube in Paris …

G.M.: … jeweils mit einer Bildlegende versehen, die Aufnahmeort und -zeit genau festhält. Sind Ihre Bilder auch Dokumentationen?

P.A.L.: Nach all der Bilderfülle, welche uns im Leben begegnet und mit der ich mit meinen vorhandenen Fotografien auch konfrontiert bin, war ich gezwungen, diese zu ordnen, auszuwählen, zu kombinieren und systematisieren. So ergeben sich viele Kapitel und Themengruppen. Gewisse Motive wiederholen sich also ständig, durch ihre Bildlegenden werden sie zeitlich und räumlich differenzierbar.

G.M.: Sie sind ein unermüdlicher Sammler. Ihre Wohnung bordet über von gefundenen Objekten, Zeitungsausschnitten … Was treibt Sie an? Sammelwut? Bildergier?

P.A.L.: Ja das stimmt. Es ist dieses Hängen an nutzlosen Gegenständen, für andere völlig wertlos. Dieses Sammeln ist eine Leidenschaft – und bei mir – auch künstlerisches Programm. Dazu kommen die Erinnerungsassoziationen, ausgelöst über einen Gegenstand. Wie gesagt, nutzlose, billigste „Souvenirobjekte" oder aber auch „Reisefundstücke" aus Nah und Fern.

In meiner Sammlung finden sich neben Gegenständen wie einem Schirmständer vom Sperrmüll aus Brooklyn, einer Holzwurzel aus dem Tal des Todes in Nevada, Baumwollresten aus Mississippi auch allerlei Zuckerwürfel- und Hotelseifenverpackungen. Es gibt eine plattgefahrene Alu-Getränkedose aus Sénégal sowie ein rostiges Stück Blech aus Vukovar in Kroatien. Es gibt Steine, Muscheln, Postkarten, Zeitungen, Kondomverpackungen, Plastiktaschen. Ja, es ufert tatsächlich aus. Dabei erwähnte ich noch gar nicht die Sammlung meiner Tonkassetten. Inhalt: Soundcollagen vieler Reisen mit einigen schönen Stellen, wie Bahnhofsgeräusche, Großstadtverkehr, Radiostimmen, TV-Werbung in fremden Sprachen, Musikgruppen im New Yorker Subway-System spielend, Gesprächsfragmente usw. …

Beim Fotografieren ist es so: Die Motive sammeln sich im Laufe der Zeit naturgemäß an. Das Œuvre wächst und wächst. Ein Ordnungssystem dabei ist, die Motive in Typologien zu ordnen. Auch das wird aber immer komplizierter. Es gibt so viele Details und Untergruppierungen.

Ein Beispiel: Ich fotografiere seit Jahren die Ambiente und Interieurs von Hotelzimmern. Innerhalb dieser Hotelzimmersujets entstanden eigene Hotelbadezimmerduschvorhangstudien. Diese Motive möchte ich alle einmal sortieren für eine Hitchcock-Thematik. Man kann auch sagen: „Alles fließt!"

G.M.: In welcher Weise intervenieren Sie in die Sie umgebende Wirklichkeit? Die Aufhebung von Erfahrungszusammenhängen, das erfahrungsgemäß nicht Zusammenhängende, Momente der Irritation und der Überraschung kennzeichnen das „Surreale". In welcher Weise ist Ihre Arbeit surreal?

P.A.L.: Durch meinen surrealen Blick. Ein übervölkerter Strand in einem Massentourismusort, ein Friedhof unbekannter Soldaten, eine riesige Hühnerfarm, ein McDonalds-Lokal irgendwo im Niemandsland … die Auflistung solcher Bilder könnte endlos fortgesetzt werden. Dank Luis Buñuels Film

Ein andalusischer Hund kann man erfahren, was Kunst vermag. Als Filmemacher würde ich sofort eine Hühnerfarm mit gackernden Hühnern besuchen, um dort zu den Klängen von Chopins *Trauermarsch* zu drehen. Der chinesische Exilautor Gao Xing Jian sagte einmal im Fernsehen: „Denn die Realität ist oft selbst absurd." Das kann ich nur bestätigen.

G.M.: Apropos „Kunst und Leben". Mir springen Fotografien von Leichen, Tierkadavern, Grabsteinen ins Auge, während Sexualität und Erotik kaum eine Rolle spielen, müsste man nicht vielmehr von „Kunst und Tod" sprechen ...?

P.A.L.: Bei einer Ausstellung im Jahre 2001 für die project wall der Kunsthalle Wien, erinnere ich mich, dass ich der Arbeit einen Satz aus einem Kirchenlied von Martin Luther voranstellte: „Mitten wir im Leben sind mit dem Tod umfangen."

Für einen Künstler ist der Tod als Thema zwingend.

Man glaubt ja gar nicht, wie stark dieser überall in unserer Kultur und Umgebung präsent ist. Ich erinnere mich weiters an das Zitat des ugandischen Schriftstellers Moses Isegawa, welcher sagte: „Wo Schönheit ist, ist auch Hässlichkeit, aber Hässlichkeit bedingt auch Schönheit."

Wieder weise ich auf mein erstes großes Buch *Kunst und Leben. Ein Roman* hin. Das Buch erschien 1999 und ich versuchte, alle meine für mich wichtigen Themen in 20 Kapiteln abzuhandeln. Neben dem Kapitel Nummer 10, welches einfach „Tiere" lautete, zeigte ich auch eine Auswahl an toten Tieren. Da hatte ich auch das Thema der Vergänglichkeit, der Verwesung, des Todesschocks dargestellt. Und dann gab es das

Kapitel Nummer 11. Dieses lautete: „Tod und Erotik (muerte y erotismo)". Multilingual verstärkt, wenn man so will. Sie sehen also, das Thema Erotik ist auch für einen Künstler stark. Wenn ich die Abbildung Nr. 129 hervorheben darf! Sie zeigt einen Ausschnitt eines Gemäldes von Antonio de Bellis (um 1640). Dargestellt ist die Figur des „Saint Sébastien". Dieses Foto entstand in Paris 1997.

G.M.: Welchen zeitgenössischen Fotokünstlern fühlen Sie sich verbunden?

P.A.L.: Arakis Arbeit hat mich sehr beeinflusst. Mit Nan Goldin, Heinz Cibulka oder Valie Export habe ich schon in diversen Gruppenausstellungen zusammen ausgestellt. Mit dem New Yorker Street Photographer Joel Meyerowitz verbindet mich seine Aussage: „I've felt the weight of the shadow." Der Schatten und seine Magie sind ein wesentliches Bildelement in meiner fotografischen Arbeit.

G.M.: Sie haben als junger Mensch eine Fotoserie mit dem Titel „Die Heimat austreiben" gemacht und sich in der Folge immer wieder vor einer auf Leinwand projizierten exotischen Reiseerinnerung porträtiert. Welche Rolle spielen Begriffe wie Heimat und Fremde für Paul Albert Leitner und sein Werk?

P.A.L.: Ja, dieser 7-teiligen Arbeit aus dem Jahre 1986 gab ich den Titel „Die Heimat austreiben". Das war in der Tiroler Bergwelt. Exakt zu diesem Zeitpunkt und in dieser Umgebung entstand diese Fotoserie. Es war ein spontanes Statement gegen die scheinheilige Umgebung und vieles andere mehr. Ein Unzufriedener rebellierte mit der Sprache der Kunst ...

Später entstand eine weitaus gelassenere, mildere Sicht des Begriffes „Heimat". Kreative Menschen haben alle die Fähigkeit, sich ihre eigenen „Heimaten" zu erschaffen. Beispielsweise die Welt der Bücher, die Welt der Kunst, die Welt der Musik können für mich „Heimaten" sein. Ich bin nun selbst erstaunt, während ich das sage, dass ich von „Heimaten", also in der Mehrzahl spreche. Was sehe ich hier: Religionen, Götter, patriotische Gefühle kommen nicht vor. Zum Thema der Fremde kann ich nur an Schuberts Winterreise denken. Auf Reisen sind wir ja immerzu mit der Fremde konfrontiert. Es ist manchmal seltsam: Ich fühle mich in der Fremde oftmals zu Hause.

G.M.: In der Ausstellung im project space zeigen Sie außer den Dias auch einige Farbfotografien. Üblicherweise montieren Sie Ihre Bilder nach einem eigenen Prinzip – dürfen Kuratoren dabei mitbestimmen?

P.A.L.: Der Autorenfotograf wählt aus und ordnet an, vom Anfang bis zum Schluss. Auch ein Autor liefert einen zu Ende geschriebenen Text ab. So sehe ich das. Meine Hängung bzw. Bilderkombination erfolgt primär intuitiv, ist also auch damit ein künstlerischer Akt.

G.M.: Urs Stahel schrieb vor knapp zehn Jahren: „Paul Albert Leitner ist eine der bemerkenswertesten Figuren in der österreichischen Fotoszene. Mit einem Anflug von gekonnter Naivität realisiert er ein vielfältiges, auch mal schräges (Foto)Programm an Selbsterforschung, in verschiedenen Konstellationen, zum Beispiel als Reisender. Zu entdecken." Empfinden Sie sich mittlerweile als „entdeckt"? Hat ihre Arbeit die ihr gebührende Position im Kunstbetrieb erreicht?

P.A.L.: Ich würde mich inzwischen als „Geheimtipp" einordnen. Ich nehme an internationalen Gruppenausstellungen teil und fühle mich in Österreich der Fotoszene zugehörig. Nach außen hin heiße ich aber noch nicht „Paul Albert Gursky".

I

Leo Kandl, Fotograf, La Habana 2001

Peter Senoner, Wien 2006

Annelies Oberdanner, Wien 2005

John Gossage, Photographer, Café Sperl, Wien 2006

Eva Maria Ocherbauer, Nähe Anhalter Bahnhof /
Askanischer Platz, Kreuzberg, Berlin 2005

Alexis Leyva („Kcho") in his studio, La Habana 1998

Raymond Pettibon, Wien 2006

Barrie Kosky, Director, Melbourne, Australia 2005

Paul Capsis, Actor (Wardrobe Schauspielhaus Wien), Wien 2002

Maryam Mohammadi, Photographer and Teacher, Shiraz, Iran 2005

Franz Blaas, Wien 2006

Mario Dalpra, Wien 2006

Ellen Cantor, Wien 1998

Walter Ebenhofer, Salzburg 2005

Rubén González in his home, Centro Habana, La Habana 1999 (†)

Antoine d'Agata (2nd International Photography Festival
Nizhny Novgorod), Nizhny Novgorod, Russia 2002

Street Photographer, 6th Avenue, Chelsea, Manhattan, N.Y.C. 2003

Shirin Neshat, Chinatown, Manhattan, N.Y.C. 2000

Christian Schwarzwald, Paris 1997

Uroš Djurić, Maler, Schauspieler, Grafiker und DJ, Wien 2006

Viktor Rogy, Aktionskünstler und Dadaist, Klagenfurt, 6. August 1999 (†)

Walter Niedermayr, Teheran, Iran 2006

Klemens Ortmeyer, Architekturfotograf, Café Okerterrassen,
Braunschweig 2007

II

Babak Zirak, Journalist and Photographer, Esfahan, Iran 2006

Susanne Moser, Semmering, Niederösterreich 1996

Roger Theodor Kühne, Chelsea, Manhattan, N.Y.C. 2003

Sandra G., Wien 2000

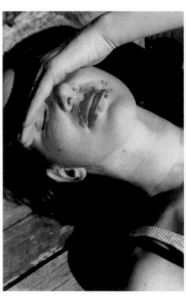

Katti Krusche, Wien 1997

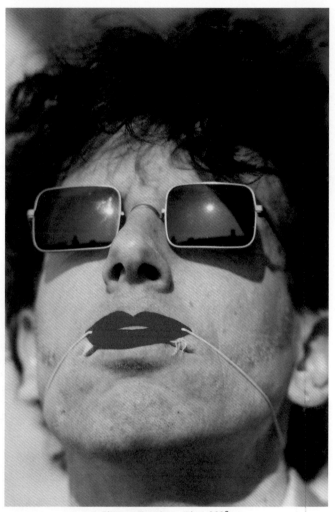

Thomas Kuscher, Wien 1998

Christine E., Wien 2006

Claudia B.,
Frankfurt am Main 2000

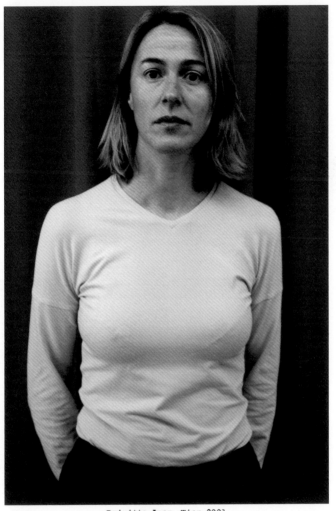

Brigitte Juen, Wien 2001

Eva Christine Jussel, Sarah Vaughan betrachtend, Wien 1999

Eduardo Rosillo, im Studio von „Radio Progreso",
Moderator der Sendung „Un Domingo con Rosillo",
La Habana, 5. Dezember 1999

André Mawazo-Mukalay, Wien 2006

Walter Joebstl, Teheran, Iran 2005

Hasti Tabatabaie, Student, Yazd, Iran 2005

Nariman Mansouri Broudjeni, Yazd, Iran 2005

Wolfgang Koch, Journalist und Autor, Wien 2006

Kristina Meret Juen, Weintraubengasse, Wien 2005

Angela Stief, Wien 2003

Maria Haigermoser, Wien 2006

Gerald Matt, im Lift des Hotels Giuseppe Tartini, Piran, Slowenien 1997

III

Selbstporträt („Berliner Schatten") Hafenplatz, Berlin-Kreuzberg 2005

Selbstporträt („Die Erde dreht sich I"), Wurstelprater, Wien 2007

Selbstporträt („Die Erde dreht sich II") Wurstelprater, Wien 2007

Self-Portrait, Club Social y Deportivo Austria,
San Isidro (Buenos Aires), Argentina 2005

Hôtel Al-Afifa, Dakar, Sénégal 2001

Self-portrait, Club Social y Deportivo Austria,
San Isidro (Buenos Aires), Argentina 2005

„Estancia El Cometa", Elisa, Argentina 2005

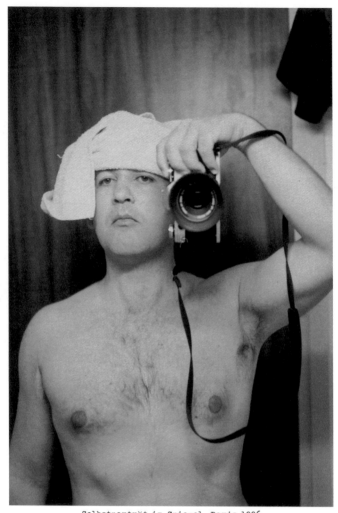

Selbstporträt im Spiegel, Paris 1996

Teheran, Iran 2006

Self-portrait, Maitland, Florida 2004

Maitland, Florida 2004

Self-portrait, „The Breakers", Palm Beach, Florida 2004

Maitland, Florida 2004

Hotel Volzhskiy Otkos, Room Number 341, Nizhny Novgorod, Russia 2002

Wien 2000

„Me, Myself in a Hotel", Gramercy Park Hotel,
Suite Number 1521, Manhattan, N.Y.C. 2002

Port Phillip Bay, St. Kilda, Melbourne 2005

„Me, Myself in a Hotel", Hotel Volzhskiy Otkos,
Room Number 341, Nizhny Novgorod, Russia 2002

Wien 2006

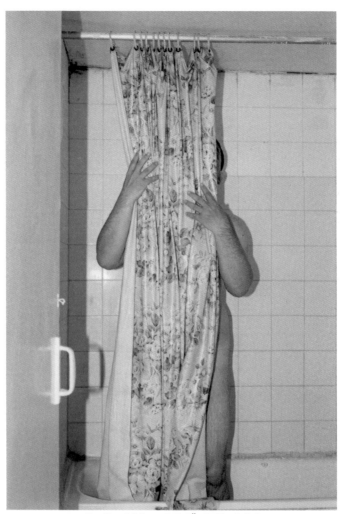

„Me, Myself in a Hotel", Julfa Hotel,
Room Number 216, Esfahan, Iran 2006

St. Lorenz am Mondsee, Österreich 2005

Selbstporträt, Persepolis, Iran 2006

Esfahan, Iran 2006

„Me, Myself in a Hotel", Gramercy Park Hotel,
Suite Number 1521, Manhattan, N.Y.C. 2002

Caspian Sea, between Ramsar and Chalus, Iran 2002

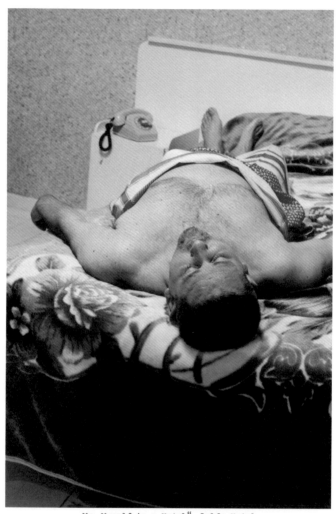

„Me, Myself in a Hotel", Julfa Hotel,
Room Number 216, Esfahan, Iran 2006

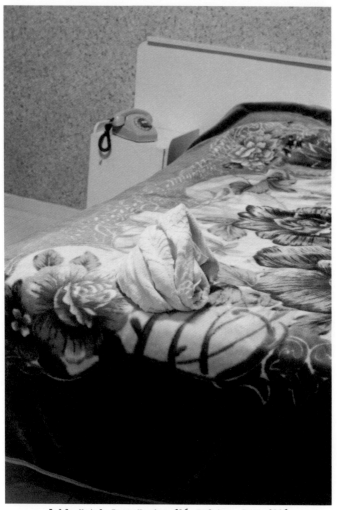

Julfa Hotel, Room Number 216, Esfahan, Iran 2006

Selbstporträt, Privatapartment Avenida Brasil,
San Telmo, Buenos Aires, 2005

Palm Beach, Florida 2004

Self-portrait, Club Social y Deportivo Austria,
San Isidro (Buenos Aires), Argentina 2005

On the way to Masuleh, Province Lahidjan, Iran 2002

Selbstporträt, Hotel Giuseppe Tartini, Piran, Slowenien,
Sonntag, 9. Februar 1997, gegen 9 Uhr 20 Minuten

Melbourne 2005

„Me, Myself in a Hotel", Tehran Kowsar Hotel,
Room Number 404, Tehran, Iran 2006

Wien, 3. April 2002

Self-portrait, Bucharest — Titan, 2006

Bucharest — Titan, 2006

Selbstporträt im Badezimmerspiegel,
Zimmer Nr. 125, Hotel Majestic, Tunis 1999

Gammarth, Tunesien 1999

Foreword

It is only shallow people who do not judge by appearances. The true mystery of the world is the visible, not the invisible.

Oscar Wilde

Paul Albert Leitner certainly has an eye for the mysteries of the visible. He presents it in all its crudeness and takes the viewer with him on a journey through the world. The realism of his work is striking; but far from being coolly documentary, it is artificially heightened by precise *mises en scène*. In this way, a second reality is superimposed over the immediately visible, revealing its other face—be it funny, cruel, desiring, or decadent. The apparent distortions of the real caused by composition, focus, and color serve a poetic intensification and analysis of the world.

For his exhibition in the project space at Kunsthalle Wien, Paul Albert Leitner has selected three groups of works on the theme of the portrait: *Portraits of Artists* and *Other People*, and *Self-portraits and Nature*. The sitters pose sometimes as they see themselves, sometimes according to Leitner's instructions. Composition, light, shadow, clothing are used alternately as important attributes to lend those portrayed an unsuspected reality—a reality Paul Albert Leitner identifies as their own, or which he would like to imagine as their alter ego. Then there are the pictures bearing the peculiarly dry label "Portraits of Other People"—well-known, unknown, people the artist meets on his travels or just in Vienna, and who he captures photographically in a form that is usually out of the ordinary. The third group consists of his *Self-portraits and Nature*: portraits of the artist from the past 25 years juxtaposed with details from nature. For each portrait, a nature picture reveals something about the artist on his voyages of discovery through the inner and outer world. We see one artist as he stages himself in the outside world, and another as he observes himself, mostly in the intimacy of hotel rooms.

The pictures are presented in the form of slide projections, possessing something of the quality of film—a medium that exerts a magical attraction on the artist—over a soundtrack of the music that accompanies him and his photographs throughout his life. One thing a slide projection has over film is the aspect of lingering, so that contemplation becomes possible. The exhibition also includes color prints from the artist's *Self-portraits and Nature* series.

Paul Albert Leitner's tireless search for a picture of the present, especially in more remote regions, on the periphery, makes him an archaeologist of a disappearing world. With unsparing openness, he shows us the cracked reality of cities that are being overtaken by globalization on the one hand and which, on the other, are decaying before our very eyes: archaeologies of once flourishing cities that are going under, and people who succumb to this rhythm or are overwhelmed by it. This revealing gaze often reminds us of Boris Mikhaylov, so admired by Leitner, although Mikhaylov's documents of a world gone mad are rendered crueler still by his form of empathy.

Paul Albert Leitner has an affinity for the world of the

remote, the world of shockingly unreal reality. The remote also implies a love of frozen time, of suspended space. The artist—a bizarre character himself, who seems to come from another time, but who is capable of reading the present moment so precisely—forces the flow to a standstill, and he firmly refuses the frenetic pace of modern life and digital technologies. This position is made possible by his distance as an observer who stands outside but who, like a reporter, often comes up against the resistance of the real, when the police or others bar his path because he has seen something he should not have seen, even if what interested him was only one very specific, unimportant detail that spoke of poetry, and not of crude reality…

I would like to thank Paul Albert Leitner for his unstinting commitment during the preparation of the exhibition, and I am pleased to be able to pay tribute to his work of the past three decades with at least a selection from his extensive archive.

I would also like thank Sabine Folie (curator) who drove this project forward together with the artist and the team at Kunsthalle Wien, Martina Piber (production) and Robert Gebauer (technician)—a project that constitutes another step on the journey which the artist has titled: "Art and Life. A Novel."

Gerald Matt
Director, Kunsthalle Wien

Paul Albert Leitner
The boy who set out … to make a portrait of the artist as a young man.
Sabine Folie

The artist described here does not set out to learn about fear, but he does share the intrepid gaze of the young man in Grimm's fairytale, the same resistance to noticing potential dangers on his travels. Paradoxically, this fearlessness causes the dangers to retreat and they are revealed as chimeras. Monstrous encounters that would force anyone else to their knees cannot touch this youngster, but in the end he is given the creeps by a bucket of cold water with minnows in it.

Our artist possesses the same peculiarly self-centred naivety and fearlessness as the boy in the fairytale: all the real and surreal occurrences on his journey are accepted, dealt with, and meticulously recorded with the camera, initially without undue emotional involvement. What might give him the creeps, what might send a shiver down the spine of this laconic chronicler with his inner smirk, we do not know: Probably something small, something inconspicuous, something we would never have thought capable of unbalancing a parodist of grand emotions and poet of what Tadeusz Kantor calls "reality of the lowest rank." But the artist and observer of the world through the medium of the self-portrait not only keeps us at a distance, in order to perform, in his deliberate poses, the proven and exhausted expressive gestures of centuries; through the exteriority of *nature*, he also grants us access to the realm of his inner life. There, in the counterparts to his physical appearance, our artist introduces the image of nature. In this diptychal juxtaposition, it serves as a complement, as a different perspective of the self turned outwards: it is a mirror of the soul. This inner being is garish red, dense, confused, the calm lake, a broken branch, frayed palms, birds at dusk—the full repertoire of sentimental imagery.

> *Meanwhile my eye will retain*
> *an invisible rose of regret*
> *as when a bird-shadow*
> *passes over a lake*
> Philippe Jaccottet, *Airs*

Alfred Stieglitz saw the cloud photographs of his *Equivalents* series (1925–1931) as expressions of his emotional state at the moment of taking the picture; their depiction, he claimed, was apt to trigger the same emotional state in the viewer.

This development, of seeing nature and the world in general as a system of correspondences, as mutually reflecting forces and not as normative, absolute facts, began in the 18th century when art and history began to reflect on their historicity, when the heroes of the classical age disappeared, and the strategy for not succumbing to desperate melancholy consisted of empathy. Friedrich Schiller's formula: "The opposite of naive perception is reflective understanding, and the sentimental frame of mind is the result of the endeavour, even under the conditions of reflection, to recover naive perception with regard to the content. This would occur through the fulfilled ideal, in which art encounters nature again."[1]

Returning from these Elysian fields of the soul to the portrayals of the artist "he, himself," we see a flaneur between worlds. When he sets off to explore far-off places, he takes his essential props with him, including a suit. In Iran, Cuba or Argentina, it is colonial white; in Romania, Persepolis, Novgorod or New York it may be grey, perhaps with a hat, mischievously commented on in *Selbstporträt (romanesk), Dachterrasse des Hotel Palace, Constanta* (Self-portrait (romanesk), Roof terrace of Hotel Palace, Constanta, 2001). The commentary "romanesk" refers to the element of re-enactment, of travesty, of simulated authenticity, of pretending: "I is an other." Labelling the self-portrait "romanesk" implies an exotic practice: a practice of appropriation and overdrawing, of typification, a characteristic of the burlesque: "...burlesque prefers rigid types on account of their striking character. The drunk, the foolish farmer, the boastful soldier and the miser are all figures that constantly recur."[2] The term "romanesk"

---

1 Friedrich Schiller, *On Naive and Sentimental Poetry*, 1795

2 Wilhelm Fraenger, *Formen des Komischen*, Dresden, 1995, p. 37 [transl. NG]

Selbstporträt (romanesk),
Dachterrasse des Hotel Palace,
Constanta, 2001

is used here as a kind of neologism, adapted from a foreign language to have a second meaning of epic, sweepingly novel-esque: "Life as a Novel".[3]

These obvious self-portraits feature different ways of looking at the artist's own self: intimate or distanced. The intimate portraits, mostly in hotel rooms, naked, with a towel, a turban *à la Marat,* or in the shower, resemble the famous morning face-check in the mirror: slightly melancholy, analytical, not always from the best side, seemingly unobserved views of the protagonist's back, and then the popular topos of the multiplied gaze into the mirror with a camera—the paradigm of the photographic self-portrait. This is supplemented, off to one

---

3 In Rumanian, 'romanesc' means 'Rumanian'; in germanised form, it refers to 'Roman,' the literary novel.

Jacques Louis David, Death of
Marat, 1793

Selbstporträt im Spiegel,
Paris 1996

side, by an even deeper look into the soul, as embodied in
nature: the saturated pink of the bougainvilleas quaking with
turmoil and desire; pastel greenish-blue as the background
for black splashes of shadow, a tachist sea of indefiniteness.
A system of correspondences and paraphrases, what Jacob
Burckhardt would call *equivalents*, compositional principles
that create accents, meaning and balance in the picture. Here,
vertical, horizontal or diffuse lines and outlines *in nature* often
seek a significant, formal, metaphorical correspondence *in the
portrait.*

The artist, then, photographs himself in the mirror: laconic,
coquettish, or serious, even imitating pathetic gestures, and
thus often approaching caricature. Especially since the 17th
century, artists' mirror self-portraits have questioned their sta-

tus as documenters of the real and as illusionists of the ideal. Their self-portrait—often, as in the case of Annibale Caracci (ca. 1604), one they have just completed and which features in the picture as such—has the function of self-reflection. Victor I. Stoichita speaks of the self-aware image, of authorial self-insertion via a mirror: "For the painter to portray his work, the making of this work, and himself, he must imagine and accept a *schism*: being both *in* the painting and *outside* it, being at the same time both "himself" and "another". This *schism* is discussed in theoretical treatises on art. Samuel van Hoogstraeten turns it into a rule applying to every 'historical painter': he must be both a figure in his picture and an outside viewer of what the picture portrays. The element of 'doubt' ('one cannot be both *in* the painting and *outside* it, but only either there or *here*'), corresponds to a search for the possibilities of splitting.

This search manifests itself above all in the manner of dealing with the unstable and fluctuating relationship within the split authorial self between the 'I' and the 'other'."[4] What applies for the painter applies equally, in principle, for the photographic self-portrait with a mirror, of which art history has seen many since the invention of photography. When this searching self steps back out of this *schism*, we see the other 'I' before us again: the extroverted, dressed-up artist. The distanced gaze. There is an obstinacy, an innocent and simultaneously cunning insistence on following strict rituals, coolly donning slightly old-fashioned white or grey suits and striking

---

4 Victor I. Stoichita, *The Self-Aware Image: An Insight into Early Modern Meta-Painting*, Cambridge University Press, 1998 [trans. NG]

a pose either in this get-up, half-dressed or even naked. The automatic shutter release determines the element of time in these frozen gestures. The artist must painstakingly work out the position to be able to quickly get into the right place, causing the poses to look overly contrived. The results are thus not without a certain unintended humour, as their attempts to imitate and caricature historical models are often wide of the mark, transforming the pathos of the 'educational' *tableaux vivants*, as staged in the 19th century, into an at times grotesque or decadent quotation of precisely these historical models from painting and sculpture, or of the photographer himself.

If *those tableaux vivants* were already a form of staged self-reflexive thought, in the above-mentioned awareness of the protagonists' own historicity, although affirming pathos, then *this* form of quotation, mostly in the burlesque mode, goes further in its portrayal of the loss of grand forms and of grand, meaningful gestures. Here, the *pathos formulas* so emphatically studied by Aby Warburg in the 1930s are pushed into the very realm of overdrawing, of the "superlative", where the balance between extremes of "the highest excitement (pathos) or of the profoundest contemplation (ethos)"[5] fails and slides into caricature. Warburg already identified this danger in the art of the 18th century, that period so expertly described as an age of upheavals by Werner Busch in *Das sentimentalische Bild. Die Krise der Kunst im 18. Jahrhundert und die Geburt der Moderne* [The Sentimental Picture. The Crisis of Art in the 18th Century and the Birth of Modernity] (1993).

---

5 Aby Warburg, Festwesen, p. 79, quoted in Ernst H. Gombrich, *Aby Warburg. An Intellectual Biography*, London 1970, p. 179

Gilbert & George—admired by our artist, but not in fact kindred spirits—strictly reject irony, being more likely to espouse the ideal of the pathos formula. Out of the frozen movements of the *Living Sculptures*, it should be possible to gain ontological insights, to distil the intrinsic, the essence of the true motivations, the emotions within: "I think that what we have in all the pieces, from the beginning to the end, is this image of people standing still, as still as possible in the world. Frozen. Not too much walking. We want them frozen for ever. In all our images we have that. We have these images of us, people, human beings, who have been frozen. Because only when they are frozen can you look at them. If they start running you cannot look at them. We want to make them more and more still, and more and more you can actually look at them. You can look inside them."[6]

Mere irony, however, would also be the wrong category for our artist: too much reflection would rob the sometimes amazed Don Quixote of his innocence in the face of the strange things he is forever encountering.

The artist's pedantry in his choice of colours, of subject matter, of framing, of the formal and compositional qualities obscure any emotional involvement. If there is any such involvement at all, then it is twisted into the comical, with the ironic distance of quotation, be it David's *Death of Marat* (1793), Tischbein's *Goethe in the Roman Campagna* (1787), Mantegna's foreshortened *Dead Christ* (1480) or a laurel-wreathed Dante in elegiac profile. "*Parody,*" we are told by the

---

6 Gilbert: "Interview with David Sylvester", in: *The Rudimentary Pictures*, Milton Keynes 1998, unpaginated

Johann Heinrich Wilhelm
Tischbein, Goethe in the
Roman Campagna, 1787

Selbstporträt, Forum
Romanum, Rom 1999

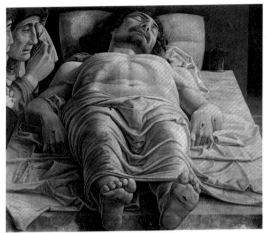

Andrea Mantegna, Dead Christ, 1480

scholar of the comical, Wilhelm Fraenger, "jokingly keeps the elaborate, noble forms of the mocked original, but intersperses them here and there with trivial details."[7] The echoes of the original are more or less evident, but mostly knocked off their sublime pedestal into the trivially human or the nostalgically elegiac—as in the many scenes where the protagonist lies stretched out corpse-like on a bed.

There is no *punctum*—the emotional impact caused by a chance element, as described by Roland Barthes—that touches or moves the viewer. The artist is not aiming for empathy or the sentimental in the Schillerian sense, although these qualities seem to shine through at times. The protagonist withholds his sentimental education from us; we can guess at it, as the

---

7 Fraenger, op. cit., p. 56

„Me, Myself in a Hotel",
Gramercy Park Hotel,
Suite Number 1521, Manhattan,
N.Y.C. 2002

photographic anamnesis takes us back 25 years, landing the
"artist as a young man," not very heroic, wearing a blanket
and sunglasses, in the swimming pool. He stands there up to
his knees in the water, unlikely to become an object of desire
for David Hockney. Years later, the same anti-hero stands in
a white suit on the diving board next to the pool, the other
half of the portrait shows the same scene—the hero has van-
ished—with a dog moving towards the diving board. From the
portrait of the artist as a young man to the portrait of the artist
as a dog—this is the kind of self-irony preferred by our mis-
chievous artist. Not so Gilbert & George, whom he sometimes
seems more to parody than to quote in his frozen gestures: "We
are living sculptures. All the good ones for us are living monsters, like Van Gogh. He became a living sculpture. Don't you

Selbstporträt mit
Lorbeerkranz, Wien 2000

think even Rembrandt became a living sculpture, or Francis
Bacon became a living sculpture?"[8]

This artist is interested in the profanation of the sacred, of
the sublime, but also in the rehabilitation of the grand gesture
that no longer seems appropriate, has become cracked, sur-
viving only in the form of parody, if at all. This sphere of the
sublime has been thoroughly explored, and it seems there is
no corner left where the artist could present himself with any
dignity, because ridicule is lying in wait to dispel any sign of
pathos.

On his *sentimental journeys*, then, the artist keeps a journal
in the medium of photography. In it, he records the transfor-
mations he undergoes in the course of his voyage through life.

8 Gilbert & George, in: *The Rudimentary Pictures*, op. cit.

Entirely in the tradition of Lawrence Sterne's *Sentimental Journey through France and Italy* (1768) and the many subsequent novels of personal development through travel, the artist sets off (as a young man) on a journey into his own self. His perception passes through the autobiographical form of his outer, physical existence, juxtaposed in diptych form with nature as a mirror of the soul. Experience of the outer world is intended to bring catharsis, very much in the sense of Goethe's *Italian Journey* (1786) or Tieck's *Franz Sternbald's Wanderings* (1798).

Since the advent of ethnographic study, journeys of this kind no longer exist, as Claude Levi-Strauss grumbles in *Tristes Tropiques* (1955): "Journeys, those magic caskets full of dreamlike promises, will never again yield up their treasures untarnished. A proliferating and overexcited civilization has broken the silence of the seas once and for all. The perfumes of the tropics and the pristine freshness of human beings have been corrupted by a busyness with dubious implications, which mortifies our desires and dooms us to acquire only contaminated memories."[9]

This knowledge of the impossibility of innocence and the nostalgic is combined with distortion into the helplessly ridiculous. The result is caricature. There is no place for sentimentality: the logic of globalism stands in stark contrast to the cracked self, as if the latter were a relic from bygone times—whether its presents itself as jovial, stiffly suited, or soft and vulnerable in a state of semi-undress.

Perhaps only music is truly nostalgic—the music of bygone

---

9 Claude Levi-Straus, *Tristes Tropiques*, trans. John & Doreen Weightman, Penguin Books 1992, p. 37f

times which accompanies the artist and his pictures as a resonator of memory and as the filling of a theatrical space that almost becomes cinematic. It offers comforting fatigue, and now and then maybe a little ecstasy …

The documentarist with the surreal eye.
Paul Albert Leitner interviewed by Gerald Matt

Gerald Matt: You always say: "The best speed for a photographer is walking pace." Is slowness an essential part of your artistic strategy?

Paul Albert Leitner: I think so, yes! It's my attitude. That's the way I am. One day, the wisdom that comes with age showed me that speed is an illusion and that so-called turbo-capitalism is something ridiculous. Maybe the reason why sport has never really fascinated me is because all that counts is competing against mechanically measured time. The Marschallin's philosophizing in Hofmannsthal's *Der Rosenkavalier*, what the quantum physicist Anton Zeilinger said; or Albert Einstein's idea that speed depends on one's own movement or the gravitational field in which one finds oneself—all these aspects of time and its passing have already been discussed elsewhere! [1]

More and more, I am an observer. Contemplation and observation take time. I stand on the periphery as a sceptic. I have to protect myself from the crowd. I'm always reminded of herds of sheep. "Redeem the time, because the days are evil." (Epistle to the Ephesians).

But back to photography and the slowness of time. My motifs—in the countryside as in the city—are obtained by walking. Often, this also involves physical pain. Pain and patience. Sometimes luck. The luck of chance. I would like to note a passage from the Neue Zürcher Zeitung newspaper from May 19, 2007, on exactly this theme of 'slowness.' I read a sentence by Walter Benjamin: "The labyrinth is the home of the hesitant." From which Hartmut Böhme concluded: "The flaneur does not seek the quickest path from here to there, preferring instead the odysseys of chance." How relevant to me and my working method. I'm afraid it also occurs to me to mention that it is becoming increasingly difficult to stroll through city streets. The reason for this is the crazy cyclists on their 'cycle paths' for which the sidewalks have simply been cut in half.

G.M.: Robert Musil is quoted as having once said: "My ear stands on the street like an entrance." Paul Albert Leitner might say, "My eye stands on the street like an entrance." Or am I mistaken?

---

1 See Gerald Matt's interview with Paul Albert Leitner in the exhibition catalogue for *Vertigo* at the Ursula Blickle Stiftung, Kraichtal, published by Triton, Vienna, 2001.

P.A.L.: Both statements apply to me, but in the reverse order, and mostly only after a movement, the movement of walking the streets with my eye. When I explore a place that is new to me, my eye is at first an "entrance" moving at walking pace, an entrance that only stands still when a situation or constellation presents itself that I want to include in my archive, entry to which is then granted by means of my camera. Sometimes the situation may be connected with sounds that belong with the picture. I record these sounds with a dictaphone. The screeching tires of braking busses on New York's Madison Avenue sounds like a piece of avant-garde music. At a moment like that, both my eye and my ear stand on the street "like an entrance." Later, I combine the pictures and recordings in slide-sound collages.

G.M.: In the exhibition at the project space, you have installed several image-and-sound collages. What does the visitor hear?

P.A.L.: The exhibition consists of three themed groups of slides projected in sets of 80 images, plus a selection of prints hung on the wall. For this particular situation, I specifically want to create an atmosphere that comes close to the film medium. Which is why this time, rather than using dictaphone field recordings, I'll be putting together a collage of my own using various pieces of music, music I like and listen to often. It will be a mix of world music, jazz, classical, Maria Callas—my favorite opera singer—Ibrahim Ferrer, Frank Sinatra, and others. This music provides an acoustic carpet for the exhibition space, while a total of 240 slides succeed each other on the walls. I don't make films, but I love film and the cinema as an atmospheric space.

G.M.: Apart from a series of self-portraits taken on your travels, we will also see "portraits of other people". These include personalities like John Gossage, Shirin Neshat or Katarzyna Figura, but also anonymous figures. How do these portraits come about?

P.A.L.: For many years now, the overall title of my photographic work has been: "Art and Life—A Novel". Much of my life takes place on journeys. Wherever I happen to be, I see things, situations and moments arise which I then photograph. This is also the way I meet the subjects of my portraits. They may be people I don't know on the street or in a café who I wish to capture in a photograph, but they can also be internationally renowned artists or musicians, for example, or curators and museum directors. Some of them I already know beforehand, having worked with them on my exhibitions, which are often group shows, others I only know by name. I never 'hunt down' a particular 'star' to get them in my collection; I meet them. So my portraits are not snapshots. A portrait requires the agreement of the subject before work can begin in the photograph. You just mentioned the well-known Polish actress Katarzyna Figura: I was spending the New Year's Eve of the millennium at the Sopot Grand Hotel on Poland's Baltic coast. In an overcrowded café in Sopot, a couple sat down at my table, it was

Katarzyna and her friend Kai. That's how I met her. A year later, we met up again in Warsaw.

> G.M.: Your portraits often appear staged, either because of the sitter's posture or because of certain 'props.' How is it possible, on the basis of a chance meeting on your travels, to achieve the necessary peace for a kind of 'studio shot' without a studio?

P.A.L.: The 'studio' is the setting in the given situation, from which I sometimes borrow a 'prop,' a piece of colored fabric or a spiky chestnut. Objets trouvés, so to speak. As I said, the person has agreed to have their portrait made. So they follow my stage instructions or spontaneously contribute their own ideas. Mostly—as with Helmut Newton—the rule applies: Don't move! But only at the moment of taking the picture, of pressing the shutter release. The 'picture' comes into being beforehand, in my imagination, and takes shape within its setting before the shot is actually staged. 'Setting' means not necessarily the specific location where I meet the person, but rather the broader ambience of that location. Sometimes there are clichéd backgrounds like a terrace with a view or a twilight mood. Lighting is very important for staging, atmosphere and composition, which may result from light and shadow.

> G.M.: What do you consider to be the role played by the *tableau vivant* here? Do you restage quotations from art history? Your self-portrait in the Forum Romanum inevitably recalls Tischbein's portrait of Goethe. Or the Tyrolean

collector Lothar Tirala posing like one of Erwin Wurm's *One-Minute Sculptures* ...

P.A.L.: Yes [laughs], these things sometimes happen of their own accord. Leitner as Goethe in Rome, that was deliberately staged as a quotation, of course. But the portrait of Tirala was taken in 1997, in Istanbul, at a time when I was not yet aware of Erwin Wurm's staged situations. But sometimes I have a spontaneous association, and then I paraphrase a picture that comes to mind. For example, I photographed Klemens Ortmeyer in profile so that only one eye is visible, like in Irving Penn's 1957 portrait of Pablo Picasso. But in Penn's photograph, Picasso's eye looks at the viewer, whereas Ortmeyer is wearing sunglasses. So these are not really *tableaux vivants* that I stage when an existing picture occurs to me, it happens more associatively.

G.M.: Paul Albert Leitner in hotels: a constantly recurring subject. The hotel room as a 'studio' from New York to Montevideo ...

P.A.L.: ... or as a special stage for my self-portraits when traveling. When I travel, I always take my eggshell-colored "photo suit" with me, and I always take a self-portrait in this suit at the hotel. On the one hand, this captures a momentary state, and on the other, I create a document of my existence. By always appearing in the same suit, I highlight the fact that my work is not so much about the locations where the pictures are taken as about the question of "Art and Life": a character out of novel, I appear here and there, and a hotel room means something like a temporary residence, a short stop on the way. I call these self-portraits "Me, Myself in a Hotel". There is a quotation here too, incidentally: a picture by Max Beckmann from 1922 entitled *Selbst im Hotel* (Self in a hotel).

G.M.: If we're talking about the same picture—I know a lithography with that title—then it shows Beckmann smoking a cigar. The smoking motif occurs frequently in your portraits, too.

P.A.L.: In the past, the cigarette was practically a fixed 'attribute' of the artist, a symbol of individuality, independence, self-confidence. Then almost everyone started smoking, a cigarette was no longer anything special. But today, smokers are being marginalized, "smokers cause lasting damage to themselves and those around them," written on every packet of cigarettes. This means that declaring myself a smoker in a portrait now has a special dimension again. This is why I'm interested in this 'motif,' although personally I very seldom smoke. But I also 'collect' other motifs, such as gold teeth in a person's laughing mouth or red-painted lips—in these cases of course, it's also very much about color, about accents.

G.M.: To me, your pictures also seem to be a collection of fragmentary ideas, brief reports, fragments and essays from a world that we think we know but which we have never seen in this way before. Do you think of yourself as a storyteller?

P.A.L.: The world proposes many fascinating stories: crazy, funny, blood-curdling, excruciating, melancholy. The photographic motifs are little windows onto the world, visual splinters. The fragmentary has a great appeal for me. Fragments of an unfamiliar city, exotic plants, the beauty of a wretched power socket in a hotel room, a stranger's vomit on the street, a freshly run-over pigeon in Paris, …

G.M.: … each with a caption recording the exact time and place the picture was taken. Are your pictures also documentations?

P.A.L.: After the wealth of images that we encounter in life and with which I was also confronted in the form of my existing photographs, I have been forced to order, to select, to combine and systematize. This results in many chapters and themed groups. So certain motifs recur constantly, the captions distinguish them in time and space.

G.M.: You are an untiring collector. Your apartment is overflowing with found objects, newspaper clippings … What drives you? Collecting mania? A craving for images?

P.A.L.: You're right, I love these useless objects that other people consider totally worthless. This collecting is a passion—and it's also part of my artistic program. And then there are the memories associated with specific items. Like I said, useless, very cheap 'souvenirs,' but also things found on my travels, things from near and far.

Besides objects like an umbrella stand found on the street in Brooklyn, a tree root from Death Valley in Nevada, and scraps of cotton from Mississippi, my collection also includes all kinds of sugar cubes and hotel soap bars. There is a flattened aluminum drinks can from a road in Senegal and a rusty piece of metal from Vukovar in Croatia. There are stones, shells, postcards, newspapers, condom packets, plastic bags. It really is getting out of hand. And I haven't even mentioned my collection of tape recordings, containing sound collages from many journeys with a few good passages like railway sounds, city traffic, radio voices, TV advertising in foreign languages, groups of musicians playing in the New York subway, fragments of conversations, etc. …

That's how it is with photography: over time, it's natural for motifs to build up. One's œuvre grows and grows. One system is to order the motifs typologically. But even that gets more and more difficult. There are so many details and sub-categories.

One example: for years now, I've been photographing the ambience and decor of hotel rooms. Within this hotel room category, a whole series of hotel bathroom shower curtain studies has emerged. At some point, I would like to bring all these pictures together for a Hitchcock theme. One could also say: "Everything flows!"

G.M.: In what way do you intervene in the reality that surrounds you? The abolition of familiar frameworks, the experience of incoherence, elements of irritation and surprise, these are characteristics of the "surreal". What is surreal about your work?

139

P.A.L.: The way I look at things—my surreal eye. An over-crowded beach in a tourist resort, a cemetery for unknown soldiers, a gigantic chicken farm, a McDonald's restaurant in the middle of nowhere... the list of such images could go on for ever. Luis Buñuel's film *An Andalusian Dog* allows us to experience what art is capable of. As a film-maker, I would immediately visit a chicken farm with clucking chickens and shoot footage to go with Chopin's *Funeral March*. The exiled Chinese writer Gao Xing Jian once said on television: "Reality itself is often absurd." I can only agree with him.

G.M.: Apropos "art and life". I've noticed more photographs of corpses, dead animals, gravestones, while sexuality and the erotic hardly feature. Wouldn't it be more appropriate to speak of "art and death"...?

P.A.L.: For my exhibition in 2001 for the project wall at Kunsthalle Wien, I remember that I prefaced my work with a line from the funeral service: "In the midst of life we are in death". For the artist, death is an obligatory theme.

It's hard to imagine what a strong and ubiquitous presence death is in our culture, all around us. I am also reminded of something the Ugandan writer Moses Isegawa said: "Where there is beauty, there is also ugliness, but ugliness also presupposes beauty."

Here I would refer again to my first major book "Art and Life: A Novel." It was published in 1999 and I tried to deal with all the themes that are important to me in twenty chapters. As well as Chapter 10, simply titled "Animals," I also included a selection of dead animals. So I also covered the theme of transience, of decay, of the shock of death. And then there was Chapter 11. Its title was: "Death and Eroticism (muerte y erotismo)". Multilingually reinforced, one might say. So you see, the erotic is also a strong theme. If I might point to Fig. 129! It shows a detail from a painting by Antonio de Bellis (circa 1640) of Saint Sebastian. This photograph was taken in Paris in 1997.

G.M.: Which contemporary art photographers do you feel close to?

P.A.L.: I have been very influenced by Araki's work. I have shown work in various group shows with Nan Goldin, Heinz Cibulka, and Valie Export. I concur with the New York street photographer Joel Meyerowitz when he says: "… I've felt the weight of the shadow". Shadow and its magic are a key visual element in my photographic work.

G.M.: As a young man, you made a series of photographs with the title "Exorcizing the Homeland" and since then you have repeatedly made self-portraits against projections of some exotic travel memory. What role do concepts like "home" and "abroad" play for Paul Albert Leitner and his work?

P.A.L.: Yes, I gave a seven-piece work from 1986 the title "Exorcizing the Homeland". It was in the mountains of Tyrol. That was the exact time and place where this series of photographs was made. It was a spontaneous statement against that sancti-monious setting and much more besides. A malcontent rebel-ling with the language of art…

Later, I developed a milder, far more relaxed view of the concept of "homeland". Creative people all have the ability to create a "homeland" of their own. For example, the world of books, the world of art, the world of music can be "homelands" for me. As I say this, I am astonished to hear myself talking of "homelands" in the plural. What do I see here: religions, gods, patriotic feelings do not feature. On the theme of "abroad", what occurs to me is Schubert's *Winter Journey*. When we travel, we are constantly confronted with the unfamiliar, the foreign. Sometimes its weird: I often feel at home when I'm abroad.

G.M.: In the exhibition in the project space, apart from the slides, you are also showing a number of prints. You usually hang your pictures according to your own principles—do curators have any say in this?

P.A.L.: The auteur photographer is responsible for the selection and the arrangement, from start to finish. Just like a writer sub-mits a finished text. That's how I see it. My hanging, the way my pictures are combined, is based primarily on intuition, which means it is an artistic act.

G.M.: Ten years ago, Urs Stahel wrote: "Paul Albert Leitner is one of the most remarkable figures in the Austrian pho-tography scene. With a trace of masterful naivety, he realizes a diverse, sometimes offbeat (photographic) program of self-examination, in various constellations, for instance as a traveler. Worth discovering." Do you think you have now been "discovered"? Has your work achieved the position it merits in the art world?

P.A.L.: Today I would classify myself as an "inside tip". I take part in international group shows and in Austria I feel I am part of the photography scene. But I'm not yet being referred to as "Paul Albert Gursky".

Biografie | Biography

PAUL ALBERT LEITNER

1957 geboren in Jenbach, Tirol, Österreich
1973–76 Ausbildung zum Fotografen
Seit 1986 freischaffender Künstler
Lebt in Wien

Born in Jenbach (Austria) in 1957
1973–76 Study in commercial photography
Freelance artist since 1986
Lives in Vienna

Einzelausstellungen (Auswahl) | Solo Exhibitions (Selection)

1988	„Blauer Zufall am Horizont", 18 Polaroid Inszenierungen	Stagings, Secession, Grafisches Kabinett, Wien
1989	„Weltverwirrung" (Kat. | cat.), Österreichisches Fotoarchiv im Museum moderner Kunst, Wien
1990	„Weltverwirrung", Fotogalerie im Forum Stadtpark, Graz
	„Weltverwirrung", Frankfurter Kunstverein, Frankfurt/M.
1992	„Die Reise zum Heiligen Sebastian", Galerie Niels Ewerbeck, Wien
	„Exkurs über das Reisen", Galerie Fotohof, Salzburg
	„3 x 1 + 1" (zusammen mit | together with Nan Goldin, Sandy Skoglund, Alice Springs), Fotoforum Bremen, Bremen
1994	„Die Reise zum Heiligen Sebastian", Fotoforum Bozen, Bozen
1995	„Totes Leben. Stillebenvariationen", Galerie Faber, Wien
	„Viaggo verso San Sebastiano", Galleria Libreria Agorà, Turin
1996	„Bild und Abbild des jeweils anderen. Eine Kooperation von Paul Albert Leitner und Georg Salner" (Kat. | cat.), („ferdinandeum video 10"), Studiogalerie Landesmuseum Ferdinandeum, Innsbruck
1999	„Kunst und Leben. Ein Roman", Galerie Faber, Wien
2000	„Kunst und Leben. Ein Roman" (Diaprojektion, Akustische Fragmente, Lesung fragmentarischer Notizen | slide projection, acustic fragments, reading), Magazin 4, Bregenz
	„Kunst und Leben. Ein Roman", Galerie Rhomberg, Innsbruck
2001	„À la recherche des images perdues / Auf der Suche nach den verlorenen Bildern: Dakar – St. Louis", PENCUM – Goethe, Dakar
	„Kapitel 10 ‚Tiere' aus dem photographischen Zyklus ‚Kunst und Leben. Ein Roman'", Kunsthalle wien project wall, Wien
2002	„Magie der Ränder: Kuba-Rumänien / Magia peryferii: Kuba – Rumunia" (Kat. | cat.), Österreichisches Kulturforum, Warschau

2003   Aus dem Zyklus | from the cycle „Kunst und Leben. Ein Roman"/Sarjasta „Taide ja elämä. Romaani", Hippolyte Valokuvagalleria / Photographic Gallery, Helsinki

2004   „solo show. selected photographs (Das Gewicht des Schattens)", Galerie Rhomberg, Innsbruck

2005   „Cities, Episodes. Photographs", Galerie Steinek, Wien

2006   „0–24 – Signs and Advertisements", IZBA Gallery, Novi Sad

       „Buenos Aires: Laberintos y Sueños", Galerie foto forum, Bozen

       „Magie der Ränder: Kuba – Rumänien / Magia peryferii: Kuba – Rumunia", Galeria Nouă, Bukarest

       „Recent photographs", Galerie Rhomberg, Innsbruck

2007   „Love, Death + Passion", Galerie Steinek, Wien

Ausstellungsbeteiligungen (Auswahl) | Group Exhibitions (Selection)

1982   „Neue Photographie aus Tirol" (Kat. | cat.), Galerie im Taxispalais, Innsbruck; Waltherhaus, Bozen (1983); BRG Galerie, Wörgl (1983)

1985   „Vier Wege" (Kat. | cat.), Österreichisches Fotoarchiv im Museum moderner Kunst, Wien; Budapest Galéria, Budapest (1986)

1986   „Von Wien aus", Museum für Photographie, Braunschweig

       „Ich-Bilder/Welt-Bilder", Fotogalerie im Forum Stadtpark, Graz

1987   „Fotografie in Österreich" Reihe Europäische Fotografie 2/87 (Kat. | cat.), Fotografische Sammlung Museum Folkwang, Essen

1989   „Kunst der letzten 10 Jahre" (Kat. | cat.), Museum moderner Kunst, Wien

       „Dokument und Konstrukt" Zeitgenössische Fotografie aus Österreich (Kat. | cat.), Moskau

       „Zeit-Bilder" 150 Jahre Photographie: Tirol, Südtirol, Trentino (Kat. | cat.), Museum für Moderne Kunst, Bozen; Galerie im Taxispalais, Innsbruck; Palazzo delle Albere, Trient

       „Installation – Konzeption – Imagination" Fotoarbeiten der Österreichischen Fotogalerie Rupertinum (im Rahmen des steirischen herbstes '89), Kulturhaus, Graz

1990   „Document and Construct. Contemporary Artistic Photography from Austria" (Kat. | cat.), The Gallery at The Austrian Cultural Institute, New York

1991   „45 Selbstbildnisse" (Kat. | cat.), Galerie Ziegler, Zürich

       „Im Bilde – v obraze" (Kat. | cat.), Galerie der Hauptstadt Prag; Oblastny Galerie Vysochiny, Iglau, Mähren; Minoritenkirche Krems/Stein

       „Absolutismus und Exzentrik. Die Kunst des Entschwindens – Assolutismo ed eccentricità. L'arte dello svanire" (Kat. | cat.), AR/GE Kunst Galerie Museum-AR/GE Kunst Galleria Museo, Bozen; Museo Casabianca, Malo-Vicenza (1992); Galleria d'Arte Contemporanea, Rimini (1993)

       „European Photography Award 1991", Künstlerwerkstatt im Bahnhof Westend, Berlin

1992	„Rupertinum – Fotopreis 1991" (Kat.	cat.), Rupertinum, Salzburg
1994	„FotoAlbum (Austria)" (Kat.	cat.), ARTprop 163 Mercer Street, New York
1995	„Fisch & Fleisch. Photographie aus Österreich 1945–1995", (Kat.	cat.), Kunsthalle Krems, Krems-Stein

1992 „Rupertinum – Fotopreis 1991" (Kat. | cat.), Rupertinum, Salzburg

1994 „FotoAlbum (Austria)" (Kat. | cat.), ARTprop 163 Mercer Street, New York

1995 „Fisch & Fleisch. Photographie aus Österreich 1945–1995", (Kat. | cat.), Kunsthalle Krems, Krems-Stein

„Portraits 1845 – 1995", Fotografien, Galerie Faber, Wien

1996 Antagonismes / Antagonismen, 30 ans de Photographie Autrichienne (1960–1990) / 30 Jahre Österreichische Photographie (Kat. | cat.), Centre National de la Photographie, Paris; Musée de l'Elysée, Un Musée pour la photographie, Lausanne

„Rupertinum-Fotopreis 1995" (Kat. | cat.), Rupertinum Salzburg; Fotoforum West, Innsbruck

1997 „Una visión real/Eine reale Vision", Zeitgenössische österreichische Photographie aus den Sammlungsbeständen des BMWVK Wien und der österreichischen Fotogalerie Rupertinum Salzburg, (Kat. | cat.), Centro de la Imagen, Mexico City; Künstlerhaus, Wien

Exposition Collective, Cité International des Arts, Paris

„Alpenblick. Die zeitgenössische Kunst und das Alpine" (Kat. | cat.), Kunsthalle Wien

1998 „Collezione Tirolo" (Kat. | cat.), Complesso Monumentale del San Michele a Ripa Grande, Rom

2000 „WIDERSTAND, art and politics from Austria", artspace Rhizom, Aarhus, Dänemark

„Vienna Exposed", Campus ArtGallery, Santa Rosa Junior College (SRJC), Santa Rosa, California; University Art Gallery, Cal Poly, San Luis Obispo, California (2001)

„Nicht ganz koscher?", Österreichisches Jüdisches Museum, Eisenstadt

2001 „VOR ORT I", Ideen für eine Sammlung, Galerie der Stadt Schwaz, Schwaz in Tirol

„Vertigo", (Kat. | cat.), Ursula Blickle Stiftung, Kraichtal – Unteröwisheim; Magazin 4, Vorarlberger Kunstverein, Bregenz

„medium foto buch", Galerie der Stadt Wels, Wels

„Spętani-wyzwoleni. Sztuka austriacka XX wieku / Gefesselt – entfesselt. Österreichische Kunst des 20. Jahrhunderts" (Kat. | cat.), Zachęta Państwowa Galeria Sztuki / Staatliche Kunstgalerie Zachęta, Warschau

„La natura della natura morta – fotografia. Da Fox Talbot ai nostri giorni" (Kat. | cat.), Galleria d'Arte Moderna, Bologna

2002 "Pro-vision", 2. Internationales Festival für Fotografie (Kat. | cat.), International Exhibition Center "Nizhegorodskaya Fair", Nizhny Novgorod, Russland

"Contemporary European Photography" (Kat. | cat.), Tehran Museum of Contemporary Art, Tehran, Iran; Isfahan Museum of Contemporary Art; Mirali Tabrizi Gallery, Tabriz

„Weegee The Famous" (Zusammen mit | together with Hermann Huber und Leo Kandl). Galerie Dsyga, Lemberg, Ukraine

2003 „Tirol Transfer" (Kat. | cat.), Krinzinger Projekte, Wien; Galeria BWA Bydgoszcz (Polen); Österreichisches Kulturforum, Warschau (2004)

„ZUGLUFT – Kunst aus Wien". Ausstellung im Rahmen der Kunst Zürich, 9. Internationale Messe für Gegenwartskunst, ABB Halle Zürich-Oerlikon, Zürich

„lični pogled / personal view", (Kat. l cat.), galerija ARTGET, Kulturni centar Beograda. Ausstellungsserie unter dem Titel Veza / Connection im Rahmen der II International Danube Conference on Art and Culture, Belgrade, Serbia and Montenegro

„Go Johnny Go! Die E-Gitarre-Kunst & Mythos" (Kat. l cat.), Kunsthalle Wien

2004   „Wiener Linien. Kunst und Stadtbeobachtung seit 1960" (Kat. l cat.), Wien Museum Karlsplatz, Wien

2005   „Choose a shoe", Galerie Steinek, Wien

„simultan. zwei sammlungen österreichischer fotografie aus den beständen des bundes und des museum der moderne / two collections of austrian photography. from the collections of the federal chancellery and the museum der moderne." (Kat. l cat.), Museum der Moderne Salzburg Mönchsberg, Salzburg; Fotomuseum Winterthur, Schweiz

2006   „OPERA AUSTRIA – Frammenti di prospettive. L'arte del cuore dell'Europa / Brüchige Perspektiven. Kunst im Herzen Europas" (Kat. l cat.), Centro per l'Arte Contemporanea Luigi Pecci, Prato

„Der Schuh in der Kunst", Galerie im Traklhaus, Salzburg (Kat. l cat.)

„Steady State", Fotografie, UBR-Galerie, Salzburg

2007   „die neue kollektion. ankäufe, erwerbungen und geschenke 2001–2006", Tiroler Landesmuseum Ferdinandeum, Innsbruck (Folder)

„21 Positions" (Kat. l cat.), Austrian Cultural Forum New York

Katalog- und Buchpublikationen l Catalogs and Books

„In die Ferne und nach Innen". Kat. l Cat. Fotogalerie Gabriel, Wien 1985

„Blauer Zufall am Horizont: 18 Polaroid-Inszenierungen". Mit einer Reflexion von Bruno Liberda. Hrsg. v. l ed. by Otto Hochreiter, Ariadne-Verlag, Wien 1987

„Weltverwirrung". Kat. l Cat. Förderungspreis für Fotografie 1988. Österreichisches Fotoarchiv im Museum moderner Kunst, Wien 1989

„Die Reise zum Heiligen Sebastian". Sonderzahl Verlag, Wien 1993

„Kunst und Leben. Ein Roman". Mit einem Text von l with a text by Gerald Matt. Hrsg. v. l ed. by Rainer Iglar / Michael Mauracher. Fotohof *edition*, Salzburg 1999

„Magie der Ränder: Kuba – Rumänien / Magia peryferii: Kuba – Rumunia". Texte von l texts by Thomas Mießgang, Andreas Stadler, Hrsg. v. l ed. by der Österreichischen Galerie am Österreichischen Kulturforum Warschau, Warschau 2002

„Städte, Episoden". Hrsg. v. l ed. by Rainer Iglar / Michael Mauracher. Fotohof *edition*, Salzburg 2005, Band 50

„Cities, Episodes". Ed. by Rainer Iglar / Michael Mauracher. Fotohof *edition*, Salzburg 2005, Volume 51

"Wien: Momente einer Stadt / Vienna: Moments of a City". Fotohof *edition*, Salzburg 2006, Band 66, dt / engl.

Fotografische Beiträge. Texte des Künstlers (Auswahl)
Photographical Contributions. Texts by the Artist (Selection)

Veröffentlichungen | Publications in Camera Austria, Graz. Nr. 5/81, 14/83, 18/85, 23/87, 25/88, 31-32/90, 53/95, 71/00

„15 Artists: 150 Years". In: European Photography. Nr. 39, Göttingen 1988

„Weltverwirrung. Textfragmente". In: „Weltverwirrung." Kat. | Cat. Förderungspreis für Fotografie 1988. Österreichisches Fotoarchiv im Museum moderner Kunst, Wien 1989

„Unendliche Melancholie". In: *Bildschmerz. Von der Melancholie der Fotografie.* Fotogeschichte. Heft 36. Jonas Verlag, Marburg 1990

„Das Binden der Krawatte oder der immerwährende Sonnenuntergang". Fotos von | Photographies by Paul Albert Leitner zu einem Text von | for a text by Gerald Matt. In: Wiener Zeitung „EXTRA", Wien 19. August 1994

"Arrival Saturday, 7th April 1990..." Text. In: Katalog Moscow and New York. Lomographic Society, 1994

„Exkurs über das Reisen". In: EIKON Internationale Zeitschrift für Photographie & Medienkunst. Heft Nr. 16/17 1995–1996, Wien 1996

„Bild und Abbild des jeweils anderen". Eine Kooperation von | A cooperation of Paul Albert Leitner und | and Georg Salner. In: Kat. | Cat. Tiroler Landesmuseum Ferdinandeum, „ferdinandeum video 10", Innsbruck 1996

„La Recherche photographique", Nr. 20, Printemps 1997, Paris

„Exkurs über das Reisen". In: KUNSTFORUM-DOKUMENTATION: ATLAS DER KÜNSTLERREISEN, Teil II, Band 137, Hrsg. v. | ed. by Paolo Bianchi, Kunstforum International, Ruppichteroth 1997

Fotos zum Textbeitrag von | Photographies for a text by Gerald Matt. In: „Remake of the weekend: Pipilotti Rist". Kat. | Cat. Oktagon, Köln 1998

„Wegen der Gegend. Literarische Reisen durch Vorarlberg". Hrsg. v. | ed. by Barbara Higgs und | and Wolfgang Straub. Eichborn Verlag, Frankfurt am Main 2000

„Photographie – die Sammlung". Hrsg. v. | ed. by Peter Baum. Neue Galerie der Stadt Linz – Lentos Kunstmuseum, Linz 2000/2001

Interview mit | with Gerald Matt. Katalog „Vertigo", Hrsg. v. | ed. by Gerald Matt für die | for the Ursula Blickle Stiftung, 2001 by Triton Verlag, Wien

Folder zur Ausstellung | for exhibition „Caras Vienesas – Gesichter Wiens". Centro de Arte Contamporánea Wifredo Lam, La Habana, Cuba, 2001 Kunsthalle wien project space

Fotos zum Thema | Photographies on the topic Insel Gorée, Senegal, Reportage „Pforte ohne Wiederkehr" von | by Thomas Mießgang. Literaturen. Das Journal für Bücher und Themen 11/01, November 2001

„10 Jahre Künstlerinnenmagazin". In: EIKON – Internationale Zeitschrift für Photographie und Medienkunst, Heft 36/37, 2001

Themenheft | Thematical issue: Porträt. Artist Page. In: EIKON – Internationale Zeitschrift für Photographie und Medienkunst, Helft 39 / 40, 2002

„Wegen der Gegend. Literarische Reisen durch die Steiermark". Hrsg. v. | ed. by Barbara
Higgs und | and Wolfgang Straub. Eichborn Verlag, Frankfurt am Main 2002
Fotorecherche von | Photographical inquiry by Paul Albert Leitner zu | for „Il Ritorno in
Patria – Reiseliteratur von W. G. Sebald". Quart Heft für Kultur Tirol Nr. 3/04

Impressum | Colophon

Katalog | Catalog

Herausgeber | Editors:
Kunsthalle Wien, Sabine Folie, Gerald Matt

Redaktion | Editing: Sabine Folie
Lektorat | Proof reading: Claudia Mazanek,
Sabine Folie
Übersetzung | Translation: Nicholas
Grindell
Graphik | Grafic design: Dieter Auracher
Druck | Print: REMAprint, Wien

© für die Texte bei den Autoren | for the
texts with the authors
© für die Bilder der Künstler und Galerie
Fotohof Salzburg | for the images with the
artist and Fotohof Gallery, Salzburg, Austria
© für den Katalog | for the catalog Kunst-
halle Wien, 2007, Verlag für moderne Kunst
Nürnberg
Cover: © Paul Albert Leitner, *Selbstporträt („*
Die Erde dreht sich II")Wurstelprater, Wien
2007, Courtesy der Künstler | the Artist und |
and Galerie Fotohof Salzburg

Verlag für moderne Kunst Nürnberg
Luitpoldstraße 5
D-90402 Nürnberg
Tel. + 49 - 0911 - 240 21 14
Fax + 49 - 0911 - 240 21 19
www.vfkm.de

Printed in Austria

ISBN 978-3-939738-71-8

Bibliografische Information Der Deutschen
Bibliothek
Die Deutsche Bibliothek verzeichnet diese
Publikation in der Deutschen Nationalbibliografie; detaillierte bibliografische Daten
sind im Internet über http://dnb.ddb.de
abrufbar.
Die Deutsche Bibliothek lists this publica-
tion in the Deutsche Nationalbibliografie;
detailed bibliographic data is available in
the Internet at http://dnb.ddb.de.

Distributed in the United Kingdom
Cornerhouse Publications
70 Oxford Street, Manchester M1 5 NH, UK
phone 0044-(0)161-200 15 03
fax 0044-(0)161-200 15 04

Distributed outside Europe
D.A.P./Distributed Art Publishers, Inc.,
New York
155 Sixth Avenue, 2nd Floor, New York, NY
10013, USA
phone 001-(0)212-627 19 99

Ausstellung | Exhibition

Paul Albert Leitner. Porträts von Künstlern
und anderen Personen, Selbstporträts und
Natur / Portraits of Artists, Other People,
Self-portraits and Nature
Kunsthalle Wien project space
10. Juli – 28. August 2007
July 10 – August 28, 2007

Kuratorin | Curator: Sabine Folie
Produktionsleitung | Production Manager:
Martina Piber
Texterfassung | Textrecordal:
Katharina Götschl
Presse, Marketing | Press, Marketing:
Claudia Bauer (Leitung | Head), Katharina
Murschetz, Ellie Wyckoff (Marketing)
Technik | Technique: Robert Gebauer

Die Kunsthalle Wien ist die Institution der
Stadt Wien für moderne und zeitgenös-
sische Kunst und wird durch die Kulturab-
teilung MA7 unterstützt.

Kunsthalle Wien is the institution of the City
of Vienna devoted to modern and contemporary art and is supported by the Departe-
ment for Cultural Affairs MA7.

Direktor | Director: Gerald Matt
Geschäftsführung | General Manager:
Bettina Leidl
Leitende Kuratorin | Head of Exhibitions:
Sabine Folie

DANK
Mein Dank ergeht an die porträtierten
Personen und an Andrew Phelps
                    Paul Albert Leitner

Nobuyoshi Araki, Wien 1997